Music To
Flame Lilies

Music To Flame Lilies

Megha Rao

tara
India Research Press

tara
India Research Press

Flat. 6, Khan Market, New Delhi - 110 003
Ph: 24694610; Fax: 24618637
www.indiaresearchpress.com
contact@indiaresearchpress.com

2020
Second Impression
First Published 2019

ISBN 13 : 978-81-8386-162-5

Printed and Bound in India for
Tara Press-India Research Press

For Tehillah, who always has
a prayer for me.

Prologue

In the heart of marigold smiles and sky kissed towers of London city, I find in myself a girl with incendiary sadness who is just trying to get over the death of her best friend. It is the spring of golden showers and glory lilies. My hands smell like freshly picked garden flowers and paint, bursts of yellow, hyacinth and air force blue and a pool of black like the night sky; except that my fingers aren't home to stars. They are war journals recounting an era of undoing myself and I am still lost, very lost without her.

I miss you, Kirti. I send a text.

I can feel my phone blur. All at once my eyes are waterfalls, a pair of ginger ale blurs. I have these flashbacks where I remember her like a sea of flames against a tender black ice horizon, staring back at me. Last evening, I watched the sunset and realized — if the sun can disappear from our view and still give us warmth, I know she is alive in the sky, in the air, in my heart, giving me light and watching over me. Always, always when I need hope, I hear her voice in the deepest caves of my soul.

'Finish up,' Helen says, as I touch my canvas lightly and try to make sense of my painting. The warmest mahogany eyes. Sherry dry lips, split open to reveal a delicate smile. Hair braided like a school girl. For two months now all I have painted is this childlike woman, this bundle of messed up universe, looking like she was lost inside the very world she was carrying on her shoulders. *I will never understand why you did what you did. All I know is that you were in pain and that I hate you for leaving.*

'You need to branch out, Noor,' Chloe says to me, tilting her head. Her sun locks fall on her face and for a minute she looks like Kirti. Kirti used to tilt her head like that. Chloe shrugs and walks away. 'I don't know who she is, but she's in every painting of yours.'

'She's my best friend,' I blurt out. *Was.*

You don't tell people how your childhood was robbed from you. How do I explain to them that all I ever see is her running around in open fields, naked, the sun drizzling on her brown skin like soap water; playing with marbles, stones, anything we could get our hands on; and flying kites in the forty degree death of jasmine summers? I can't explain what it feels like to have someone so close to you taken away. A good friend is the most valuable soul mate. Kirti was a gem. A soft glow. A luxury for a thunder heel like me.

*

I'm crying again, thankfully nobody is in the room anymore. This happens a lot. My face, an allegory of melancholy. I am hungry for my voice. I'm so empty sometimes. The feeling is maddening. I sit on the chair and cry for a while, and then, pack my things.

Honestly, it's too early to cry. I don't know how I've been reduced to this. But nonetheless, I am crying.

My borrowed time in the studio is over and I'm walking towards King's Cross station. My phone beeps the minute I get onto the tube, but I'm in a hurry to reach Angel. Maggie can't overexert herself, because she is sick and wants me to work with her on her new acrylic painting. Her dream is to have an art show one day, so we spend most of our time in her studio. There is no heater there and by the time we are done my legs freeze. But because it's her dream, and because I'd lay my bones down for her if she asked, I go along with it. After all, she took me in at my lowest.

All I want is to have some dinner and sleep. And when I say sleep I mean no more nightmares.

My phone beeps. A message. I know something is wrong. I never get messages, because nobody has this number. It's been months since I cut everyone off and I use it only to Skype call Baba and Amma. And they don't ever direct message me. I open my inbox and stifle a scream.

I miss you too.

It's from Kirti.

My heart, drunk and needled into alarm, laced with razor blade, cuts into itself. A rich red. Bloodied in prayer and hope.

I start calling her. Nobody picks up. My heart is racing with wheels on fire. It falls and I pick it up. I feel as tender and exposed as a raw wound. I wish someone would bandage me and take me home, but that's just a pipe dream.

By the time I reach Maggie's place I've already called Kirti's number thirty times. Her name is ticking in every nerve, alive and afire like never before. Jamie opens the door for me, but I don't move. I stand there, my eyes bomb shelters, my hands shaking from the cold. 'Grams!' Jamie yells.

I can hear Maggie coming and I feel like turning around and running. But Jamie's innocent eyes look like they've seen a ghost paralyze me and I don't want to trouble Maggie.

So I just wait there for someone to bundle me up and hold me while I cry.

There is a thunderstorm brewing inside me. Why did Kirti text me back if she was dead? Was she dead? But I'd been told she was dead. Was her family lying? Were my parents lying? But then, why wouldn't she reply to my messages for two months? I don't care now, I'm so mad at her.

For pretending to jump into the same well her mother had jumped into.

I'm scatter light on a rusting window sill. A frost pane of indigo. When did it get so difficult to breathe? My lungs feel like paper wind mills.

'Oh dear, what in the world…' Maggie is standing in front of me and I can see myself in her eyes. I look like I've dragged hell all over the front steps. 'Come in, dear. I'll make you a hot cup of tea.'

I hate English tea, but what she makes is decent. I don't want to offend her, so I nod my head. When she is in the kitchen I open the message again. *I miss you too.*

A lot of images suddenly bulldoze my dazed head. They told me she was dead.

Ash floats in the Ganges in solitude and carries the message through the clouds. *I miss you too.*

I'm dreaming her into existence now, even though I know she's not real.

Maggie is still in the kitchen and I open my Whatsapp. *Baba, I need to come home. ASAP.*

I look at it for a while, hoping it doesn't sound too impulsive. I click send.

Chapter One

Kashmir is not the same. Burhan Wani is dead and everyone is going mad. A lot of police stations are being attacked by mobs and stone pelting is rife. They say the Kashmiri Pandits are being targeted. I don't know how all this is going to affect us, but I have a feeling that it will, because Baba is Muslim and Amma is Hindu. That means we're fresh meat for collateral damage. We could be in trouble if people start fighting again. But nobody understands that we mean no harm. We are a family built on love. But our country is strange and our religions stranger. Where our mothers are murdered, there we pray.

Some of us just want a world without war. Without bad politics. Without hate and ruthlessness and brutal mouths and cruel intentions and manipulative fingers. Some of us just want to live without fear, without wondering if the colour of our complexion or the name of our religion or the lack of it would one day lure us into troubled waters. Some of us want peace, not pain; love, not loss; happiness, not hurt; to live like nothing is chasing us, to feel like nothing is tricking us, pushing us towards an order that is only going to cheat us in the end. Some of us want a promise land without greed, power struggles, competition, hatred and poison. Heaven on earth, humanity and harmony. But none of us know what will cure the world. We can only have hope.

London feels like a shelter from all of this now. Here there's no unrest, just strip clubs and casinos, metros and corporate slaves. I left home for city lights and a life outside frog wells. I never realized it was this bad. People actually live in fear here, especially during protests, shutdowns and sudden attacks.

As I comb my hair beside my grandmother's bed I wonder if growing up in Kashmir instead of Herga would have turned me different. For one, I'd never have met Kirti. Kirti, my softest shoulder to rest on.

I think about the fields I grew up in. And the stories I grew up hearing. The *yakshagaana* we always went for, giggling through plays and saving up for sweet corn. Cheap thrills that translated into nostalgia. How can anyone grow up without these? They are precious to me.

Nobody else in my family cares about Herga, the sleepy village, surrounded by the glowing paddy fields of south Karnataka.

Her perfume smells like a mix of aster and mint. Daadi is right next to me, lying on her bed with her eyes open and talking to me about Daada again, as she always does. Sometimes love is the beginning of slow death. Daada is gone with the autumn leaves he bookmarked between the pages of classic novels, and she still believes he will return. Maybe it is like how I hope Kirti isn't gone. We're all wishing the dead back to life. We're half alive and they're possessing the rest of us even when they're not around anymore. One look at the wistful expression on Daadi's face makes me think of how it's such a waste of time, falling in love. Everyone leaves in the end. I don't ever want to feel like Daadi. She misses Daada every day. And she cries every night. She is eighty years old and she cries every night, because she can't have him anymore.

'I want to go to Herga, Daadi,' I tell her quietly.

The paan on her lips is darker now. Her eyes turn into cigarette stubs as they glare at me. Her mind, dragon skin. Tongue thick with denial. She is not just displeased, she is disappointed in me. Empurpled vocals dancing in censure. Eyes like stone pillars. 'There's nobody there, Noor. There's no point going back. You belong here, in Kashmir, with your parents and me, not some foreign land.'

'Foreign land? It's my mother's hometown, and it's mine too!' I protest.

'But not your Baba's!'

This is a usual argument and Daadi never tires of it. I wanted her to talk to Baba and Amma about it, but now it is out of the question. Amma has never wanted to go back to her parents and Baba doesn't care for Herga. I miss Herga. I spent my entire childhood in Amma's parents' house, and even though Ajja and Ajji are no more, their ancestral home is still there, and I want to go back.

Kirti is there. And I want to see her.

'So you won't talk to them for me?' I ask her. She looks away, she is stubborn.

There is a sturdy goddess in her obstinacy. When Daadi says no it is the no of a hundred lifetimes. She's got jet marbles for irises and missiles for words. She wears an armour of pride, a helmet of dismissal. Her rebuff cuts me off instantly.

But I am as stubborn as her. I have already begun

thinking of my childhood, my land, where the water is sipped by the moonlight and the air is fresh from the smell of footprints in the sand and the fragrance of Hill Pepper and Doshi Laurel.

I am thinking of my being in Herga, where we're all sun drenched and tasting of wet grass. There are no skyscrapers here, no high rise buildings. Only hilltop temples and pastures and deserted roads. Muddy lanes and marshy land. Ferns sprouting between old rocks and evenings full of dance and laughter. The sounds of souls finding their way back to themselves. The perfume of good talk and kind words. A little place where everyone knows everyone and takes long, quiet walks with street dogs and ghosts. Gods striding before them like guidance. The people here, they are blessed and they are cursed. To the city lives, they are ignorant and uneducated, their tongues thick with accent. But the gods know their knowledge. They are more aware of their surrounding, because their feet are linked with the soil. Their heads don't touch the clouds, they sing to them. They are people of nature. Their relationship is of understanding, empathy and walking hand in hand with a goddess who gave them fruit, air and life. It is an equation of the deities, to be envied. It is everything the city could only dream of having. A life free of noise, a life unpolluted, a life with books, music and art, all with a view of lush forest.

I am coming, Kirti. I raid my mind for more memories, but every memory only makes me painfully aware that she's turned into one too.

I sigh and retire to bed early. I have a plan, tonight I am going to run away.

Chapter Two

When I arrive in Herga, Udupi, I am an archipelago of dark circles and sleepless nights. I took the first train out. It is the dawn of July and summer has hit us right in our water lorn throats.

The ancestral home is a mess. Dust has turned into a quilt over the ground and my feet are already dirty. There's a hovering stench, mouldy and musty. The sink stinks of dried up insides and the bed sheets are soiled. I should have known I was coming back to a haunted house. As I walk into Ajja's room I hear the clatter of pans. I almost dream of Ajja lying on his bed with his glasses resting on the crook of his nose. His Sanskrit books are intact and untouched. Ajji's room is adjacent and has a cradle made of cloth. This is where Amma was rocked, I think. Perhaps even me, but I don't know for sure. I miss them. I miss my grandparents so much. Ajja used to tell me so many stories about this place.

The old photos fascinate me. Wedding albums in the shelves, waiting to be picked and touched. In a culture of digital cameras and flashy polaroids, the black and white shots ease my antique heart. Ajja and Ajji are smiling at me and my heart melts. I want them back. I remember talking to them for the last time, it was all so sudden. They raised me into the woman I am today. All those times, running around in dresses, screaming at Ajji for brushing my hair a little too hard, refusing to eat onions and brinjal, secretly throwing away food or giving it to the dogs. Nostalgia sinks into me. Ajji, with her crooked glasses and complaints about the neighbours. Ajja, with his big books, in his study room, reading into the night with just a single lamp shade. I feel them in every step I take. The house is still breathing with their music.

Come back to me, I murmur. All of you, please just come back to me. I'm so sorry I left.

Baba calls me just as I am making the rounds and I wonder if I should answer. But I think I should at least tell them that there is nothing to worry, that I haven't been kidnapped.

'Baba?'

'Noor! What the hell?'

'I know, I know. I'm sorry. But... I don't know how to explain.'

'Where are you?'

'In Herga.'

There is a long pause on the other end. 'Baba?'

'Of all places...'

'Baba, of course I'd want to come here, I grew up here. This is another home to me, where my Ajja and Ajji lived.'

'But they're not there anymore!' he cries. 'I know what you're doing there. Come back right now. Forget that girl, she is dead, she is dead, Noor!'

'I know!' I scream into the phone. And then, I lower my voice. 'Listen, Baba. I have to do this. I don't know how to tell you how much this means to me, but... but I have to do it.'

He complains, he tries to reason with me, but by the end of it, he accepts. I know I am never going to hear the end of this. When Daadi finds out I am in Herga she will lose her mind. I know she's going to call me a *harami* for not obeying my elders. I can't care anymore. This is so important to me. I will never be at peace until I find out what happened to Kirti.

The nightmares will never stop.

*

There is a cockroach running around the house. I try to chase it out, but it starts flying. I'm going to have to clean this place. And some of the lights aren't working either. The clattering sound gets louder and I follow it into the guest room.

There is a young boy sitting on the bed.

My heart lurches. I tell myself not to panic, but I have no idea why there is a child inside this house. Is it one of the servant's sons? How did he get inside? Through a broken window perhaps, I soothe myself, but deep down I know that as run down as this house is, there are no broken windows. My heart is pounding at my ribcage like it wants out, and I'm numb.

He turns around and smiles at me. There is something beyond sinister about that smile, like puppet strings being pulled at the mouth. I try smiling back, but I can't. Instead, I say, 'What are you doing inside my house?'

'*Pokkade.*'

I've lost touch with this language, but right now I don't want to understand what he's saying. I need to speak *Tulu* if I want to ask the villagers about Kirti, if I want to ask the servants for the main keys and everything I'll ever need when I stay here. But not right now, not when a strange child is sitting across me, his skin caught in slow decay.

'*Eru ee?' Who are you?*

'Vetala.'

'Inno pudaru jado?' What is your name?

'Vetala.'

He laughs, so violently that the whole house booms with the sound. I close my ears, my chest leaping like skipping stones. Fear is an abusive lover banging on a hideout's wooden door. I feel so weak I open and give in to it. And then, he stops and slumps to the ground. He doesn't move.

I am now running out of the house, screaming, 'Gopi! Gopi!'

Ajja's trusted servant, who gave me the key to the house and lives next door with his wife and two daughters, comes running into the veranda. I am panting loudly. 'I saw something! *Jaadana sooye. Onji vetala.'*

'Vetala?'

He walks into the house and I lead him to the boy. He is still there. I'm like a leaf, dead and windblown. I have not even properly stepped into the house and things have already gone stale. Gopi looks at him and says, '*Saithaanu. Epage.*' *He is dead. He has always been dead.*

I am looking at a dead body.

As Gopi wraps the body and carries it out, he tells me that he knows this boy. He died recently from fever, that hours after his death his body went missing, right before the cremation. I don't say anything, because I am stumped. I don't know what I spoke to, but it wasn't the boy. Gopi tells me to be careful and lock the doors at all times.

I ask him if he can explain what I just saw. He tells me that sometimes spirits can possess dead bodies. I laugh and tell him these are just Herga bedtime stories.

'Thank you,' I say, as he leaves me with the other keys. My heart could win a race with the speed it is pumping at.

All those memories of my childhood, those rapturous flashbacks I was marveling at only minutes ago have been replaced by a feeling of unknown distance from Herga. All my childhood I'd been sheltered so well, I never realized I was living in a bubble of my hometown. Now I was going to find out what this place was really like.

I am alone again and I've never felt so terrified.

Chapter Three

I watch Parijat, the night-flowering jasmine, grow in the front yard. Daadi once warned me I wouldn't survive the cradled walls of rock hard culture and civilization. I can't drink the stories they tell me. Their spit and very breath are inked with these tales. Folklore is in their blood. They reek mythology. Gods and ghosts are ornate planets on their shoulders and they wear them like expensive perfume. This is the richness of this soil. But disbelief is not an option if I want to fit in.

That evening Gopi invites me to his house for dinner, because it is my first night and I haven't settled in. I grew up in this house. It's a building that has been alive for a hundred and eighty years. I have never known an ancestral house as big as this and I feel like I can't find my way back to it. I tried opening the coconut shelter earlier, but none of the keys would work. It is just another tiring day and the heat is getting to me. I am shamelessly crimson all over my amber skin and I haven't unpacked any creams and lotions from my suitcase. I'm still reeling from the shock of what happened.

Gopi's wife Arundhati is a great cook. She's made *ada dosa* and tomato chutney, a very strange dish made from hibiscus flowers and onion and my favourite, curd rice and spicy mango pickle.

Arundhati knows English well and I am grateful. She teaches English in the local school. When she sits down for dinner she tells me about Ajja and Ajji. How knotted together they were until the end. How Ajji cried when their favourite cow fell ill and Ajja walked all the way to the neighbouring village to get medicines. Ajja was a man of very few words, she said. And Ajji? Oh, Ajji loved gossip and gardening. I blush green, because she knows my grandparents better than I do.

'All of us miss them a lot.'

I nod. 'I miss them too.'

'We remember you only as a little girl with long

braids and *pottu* on your forehead. You have grown so much and turned into such a beautiful woman.'

I smile. 'Thank you,' I say graciously.

'Be careful though. Your body is hallowed ground to the ghosts here. They would love to possess you.'

My questions rise like the rungs of a ladder, I should have known they'd try to sell me all these tales. The village is a fool for good stories and people here will say just about anything.

'What?'

'I know you're thinking that this is ignorant coming from an educated person. But the things I have seen in this village make me go against my better judgment. Sometimes you can't help but believe.'

'I don't believe in all of this. I'm just here to find out what kind of mental illness Kirti had that made her commit suicide.'

Arundhati leans forward and asks me, 'What if Kirti didn't commit suicide? What if she was possessed by her mother's ghost?'

I am stone cold. 'Kirti was really close to her mother. Her death affected her a lot.'

'They say…' She looks around and clears her throat. 'They say that she spoke to her mother even after she died. That she used black magic to get to her.'

I shake my head vigorously. 'No. Kirti never went near the dark arts. She hated it and she hated her father. I know this.'

Arundhati doesn't say anything. I want to know more about all these tales that have been floating around. Why does everyone in this little village believe so much in things that are so unbelievable? What makes them put their faith in random rumours? 'Have you had any experiences? Supernatural ones I mean.'

'Not me, but Gopi has.'

I remember the corpse I saw today. It was the most bizarre thing I'd ever experienced. I still haven't shaken it away. I don't want to think anything of it.

'He was walking back home one day and it was dark. He had an oil lamp, and some oil to keep it burning. As he walked he heard a voice behind him.'

I lean forward, angry at how intrigued I am.

'*Anna, chooru enne kolle.* It says.' *Brother, please give me some oil.*

'And?'

'Gopi didn't look back. He kept walking. The voice grew louder and louder as he reached home, but he didn't look back. When he reached home and opened his container all the fresh oil had disappeared. There was not even a single drop left.'

'What if it was some stranger calling?'

'You know this village shuts down at seven. Especially at night, nobody dares to leave the house. There's no one in the streets. And certainly not in the forest. And how can you explain the oil disappearing?'

I don't know what to say to all of this. I just stare at her blankly.

'I'm not asking you to believe me. All I am saying is, just be a little careful. Make sure you stay away from any form of sorcery. Or even people performing sorcery. They are all cursed. They need to sell their souls to the worst of *bhootas* to perform the kind of magic they do. Remember that. I am sorry you lost your friend, but...' I know there is more to this. *But* is a lying word.

'But?'

'But none of us were surprised. When we heard that she jumped into the family well, we knew it was a long time coming.'

'That's such a mean thing to say,' I exclaim. I've got my guards up now.

She shakes her head. 'That whole family is cursed. It's better not to go looking for answers. It's better for you to just go back to Kashmir.'

*

On my way back to Ajja's house I hear a lot of howling and crying. It's my first night in Herga and I am already scared out of my wits.

I feel haunted by all the stories I've heard. And the only place to undo them is Kirti's family home. I don't even know who is going to be there, but I'll just have to find out. A home for the dead. Notorious for things unwritten.

Before I switch off the light in my room I look out through the window. I have always stood there before going to sleep so I could wave to Kirti. Her house can be seen from Ajja's place. It's far, but I can see shadows.

Suddenly, there is a light, and I see a silhouette.

It seems to be staring right at me.

Flustered, I close the curtains and put myself to sleep. This could all be gone in the morning.

Chapter Four

I find myself staring at creased white cotton. The front of a plain shirt. A fierce river of buttons coming undone at the collar bones. Runes on hands, the strangest tattoos. Rolled up sleeves and bare lower arms that for some unknown reason make me think of caramel skies and raspberry. I am staring into kohl eyes shining in the dawn light, and for the life of me I can't remember why I got here.

I raise my eyebrows at him, demanding an explanation. He shrugs.

'It's probably the village ghost. She put a spell on you.'

We are standing face to face, right in front of Kirti's ancenstral house. Him, a lethal watch dog, I, a failure of a trespasser.

His voice sounds like sin. A soundtrack of dreams, music to flame lilies. I've heard this voice before, and it's driven me just as insane, like a mother tongue I'd begged myself to abandon. A language of silence. Bone language. Slipping into the marrow like tailored sleeves. Arrow to the heart. Archer of the night. I should warn myself now that I am drawn to bad habits and addictions, and boys with intense eyes. Every time he blinks his lashes are arsonists. Laid back hedonists.

'I could be looking for a ghost,' I murmur. He peers at me carefully. His gaze is calculative, observant. The sun is rival to the way he is melting me.

'Let me up,' I croak, my throat burning.

'Little Noor, with scabby knees and a big bad mouth, all grown up now. I can't believe it.'

I blink. 'Who the hell are you?' There are stars colonizing his eyes as they twinkle back at me. Telltale, like they know a secret I don't.

'What are you doing back in Herga?'

'Looking for a dead girl.' I cross my arms. 'Now will you tell me how you know my name?'

'You're my sister's best friend. I've known you forever.'

My mouth falls open. 'K-Kalki?'

Now I remember, though I wish I didn't. How could anyone forget him? Even as a teenager he pickpocketed the most dauntless of hearts; fear of farmers, lover of daughters. I smile, thinking of how he was our childhood fear. His charcoal fingers tapping away buttons on school uniforms were memories brokenhearted girls carried around in their pockets. All the stories that have ever warned me of boys like him flutter back into me.

Get into that house, find what you're looking for and leave.

'Kalki,' I say.

He half smiles, but I am blabbering now. 'I… I got a text from… from Kirti.'

'I know.'

'You know?'

He leans against the bark of a tree and contemplates. 'Will you come inside? I'll explain everything.'

I'm afraid to go inside. I loved Kirti, but I hated her family. Her mother committed suicide when Kirti was eight, we were all witness to it. We'd been playing in her front yard after running in the paddy fields when we'd heard a splash. Suddenly, people were running towards their well and Krishna uncle was pulling out something that looked like a body. I will never forget the colour of the silk sari Kirti's mother was wearing that day. Red, the colour of the fresh roses we would always pick for her. The sky was bleeding into a lifeless sunset that evening.

I'll never forget the look of sheer terror on Kirti's face.

My parents hated that I hung out with Kirti, because they were scared of her family. Kirti's father was a black magician. Kirti's brother, Kalki, who was seven years older than her, already had a reputation for drug dealing, misleading young girls and dabbling in the profession his father was in. Occult fascinated him just as much as philosophy and Kirti always told me her brother had a library of books that she wasn't allowed to read. This trade was probably passed down. Luckily, Kalki had never been home. He'd gone off to boarding school and I wasn't allowed to visit Kirti during summer holidays, because he was there. Even saying his name was forbidden to me. What friendship could a young half Muslim, half Hindu Brahmin girl have with a boy whose family was of a lower caste and had its fingers dipped in the dark arts? This is what

Amma told me every time I begged her to let me go to Kirti's place.

He probably talks to ghosts. Beware of him.

It's strange. Living in London for so long had almost made me feel like a city girl whose logic didn't defy her. But deep down, something tells me that I'm still the little hillbilly who believed in the existence of all things magical. My best friend was the daughter of a black magician. She had too many encounters, and I don't think I could have escaped listening to them. I might not have experienced them first hand, but they were mine as much as they were hers. When I lost Kirti, I lost a sister.

I trudge into the house I know like the back of my hand. I have watched this house from my window for the past one week and I have seen this man watching me. I never knew who he was. I never realized it could be her brother.

'Why did she reply to my message?' I ask him, trying to fine-tune my shaky voice. 'Is she..."

'She's dead,' he states blankly and I look away. Why has everyone accepted it except me?

'And you should go back home. There's nothing here for you anymore.'

I'm anchored to a well-rehearsed protest. I am

here for my best friend, not a dismissal from some tattooed hooligan. No amount of godly body and monster heart is going to send me running home. 'I want to know why she died. She would have told me if she'd wanted to quit. And I want to know who sent that message.'

'I did,' he says.

For a few seconds I hold my breath and wish I was back in London just painting with Maggie. I miss her cosy guest room and the overpriced studio where I make the same painting over and over again. My muse never talks to me and I'm losing my mind in a place that doesn't even remember me. It stings. When he says I should go back home. As if this isn't my home.

And it stings that he said it was him who texted.

'What do you mean?'

The house is shabby and looks like it needs renovation. I know they are not rich enough for it. They have always been poor. They've made their living from exorcism and the weirdest of things. I don't know. Kirti told me so many things, but none of us knew clearly what her father was doing. We were both too young to understand.

I don't think I'd understand even now.

'I have her sim card. I use it as a dual sim. When

you sent that message my brain was all foggy, okay? I missed her and I was using her sim, and I just. I thought she was texting me. I don't know. She was on my mind.'

Rage hits me like a whirlwind, 'Didn't you see the contact?'

'I was smoking up. I was high.' He looks at me and grins. 'Now that you're a city girl I don't have to explain to you what that means.'

I roll my eyes and ignore the jibe. He can say whatever he wants in that insulting tone. I'm here to know why my best friend killed herself, not to chit chat with him. 'Are you a black magician too now? Did you even go to college?' I shoot back even though I know I'm walking right into a trap. He wants a rise out of me and I've given him exactly that, against my better judgment.

'Not UCL, of course. I'm no Noor Haque. But yes, I did.'

I can tell he's evaded my first question. Maybe I don't want to know if he's up to no good like his father. Suddenly, it dawns on me. 'How do you know I went to London?'

'Kirti told me.'

'I never knew you two were so close.'

'Mm. She spoke about you a lot.'

Or maybe you asked her about me a lot. I don't say it out loud, but it's in the back of my mind, and the thought somehow irks me more.

'So she's really dead,' I say, defeated.

'Yes.'

'Can you bring her back?'

He looks at me like I've said something silly, I probably have. 'Are you kidding me?'

I smile sadly. 'I wish. I'm sorry, I know I sound crazy.'

There's a long silence between us and I know I put it there. I don't have the nerve to speak again, but I finally ask him, 'How's Krishna uncle?'

'You don't know?'

I shake my head, bracing for the worst.

'He passed away thirteen days after Kirti did. He couldn't handle that both his wife and daughter died the same way.'

'Is that true?' I have never known Krishna uncle to be caring or affectionate at all, he ignored his wife and daughter his entire life.

Kalki laughs now. 'Of course not,' he says. 'They took him.'

'Who?'

He doesn't reply.

I inhale deeply. I can't help but look to my right. My geography is spot on. The dreaded well is still there and I'm panicking.

'That well.'

'What about it?'

I can't believe he's playing coy. 'Get rid of it. How can you live here? Where everyone died? Why haven't you even left yet? What are you doing here?'

'What are *you* doing here?' he asks me back.

I don't say anything. His eyebrows pinch together. He says, 'I'm surprised your parents even let you come back.'

I don't look him in the eye and he knows exactly what has happened.

'I see. You ran away without telling them.'

'I don't need their permission. I'm not a child.'

'You sure do look like one.'

Before I can say anything I hear a growl from

inside one of the rooms. I raise one eyebrow. 'You have a dog?' I ask him.

He shakes his head, a light smile pulling up the corners of his lips. I'm tempted to look at them a little more, because they're so perfectly shaped, but I'm more intrigued by the way his kajal smeared eyes cloud with mirth. They're dancing and they look like they hold libraries of secrets. I'm drawn to his mystery. I've really never been this wildly attracted to anyone and I hate myself for feeling this way. It's definitely not going to help my mission. But even as a fifteen-year-old boy he'd been handsome, dark and charming, with eyes as alive as sensuous poetry. But now, now he's something else. I have to be very careful.

'Not a dog.' He turns around and whispers, '*Vera, moolu bala.*' *Come here.* He's speaking in *Tulu*. And then, from the darkness walks out something so terrifying and majestic that I gasp. I'm about to run away, but as I pull back he grabs my arm and sends forty volts of electric current up my sleeve. I can't move, because he's touching me and I'm grateful he thinks I'm paralyzed by fear and not something else. He is holding me, and worse, looking at me with those eyes, and because I have nowhere else to look, I look at the creature in front of me.

'Is that a wolf?' I ask him breathlessly.

'Yes, they are,' he says, as an entire pack of them come out of the room. I scream and try to pull his hand away, but his grip is too strong. 'Don't be afraid. They can tell if you are. They're harmless.'

'What're they... doing here?'

'They're my pets,' he tells me casually.

'I think I need to leave now.'

'What! Why?'

He looks pissed, when I know I'm the one who should be mad. He's never even taken his eyes off me since the time he saw me, and I feel light headed. How dare he look at me this way, with so much want. I don't know what's deadlier, the wolves or the man.

'Why? You've got wolves for pets! And my parents always told me to stay away from people who have strange pets.'

He smirks. Dark curls coil around his ears and forehead and they look like springs I can wound around my finger. This is a funny feeling. I've never had such terrible butterflies living inside me before.

'Do you always listen to your parents? Haven't you ever wanted to do something rebellious?' he tilts his head to a side playfully. 'Or have you always been such a good girl. No wild side? And here you were saying you don't need their permission and you're all grown up now.'

I want to tell him about the London pub crawls and beer fests and random make out sessions, but I know that he's leading me to a dead end, and I'm not stupid to walk right into it. He wants to know how far he can push me, how far I will go. Or worse, I think, as my throat constricts, how bad I can get for him.

I shake the thought out of my head. This is no good.

'Good bye, Kalki.'

'Wait! You haven't even seen my snake yet.'

'Excuse me?' I glare at him. Then I see the green rope like figure slithering down his shoulder. I let out a cry of surprise and fall back. He takes the creature by its middle and wounds it around his arm. I am still screaming inside my head.

'Thanks for the... exhibition. You've got great stuff, but I've got to go.'

'Come on!' He spreads his arms wide. This is risky and undoubtedly unsafe for me. 'I can be your new friend. You're lost here anyway. And you've probably already heard so many horror stories that you're dying to get out of your old house.'

'Are you suggesting that I live with you? Next to... that horrid well?'

'Sure. We need to rise above all inhibitions and coexist with the things around us.'

'You're not serious!'

'You need to broaden your mind a little. The well didn't do anything to you. Detach yourself from the objects or situations that cause you grief. If someone threw me under a bus, should I feel angry at the bus? Not really.' He shrugs. 'You went to UCL, your fancy libraries should've had Kant's works.'

'Immanuel Kant?' I knew absolutely nothing about him except that he was sick, poor and a radical. 'What about him?'

'He had this interesting question. Are we living in an Age of Enlightenment or are we part of the Enlightened Age? One can never tell.' He sighs dramatically and suddenly grows serious. I know he's only doing all this to get my attention, get me to stay longer.

I almost want to laugh and ask him, 'is that what you call flirting? Talking about dead philosophers?' But I don't think I want to tease him and lead the conversation somewhere else. I'm already on shaky foundation.

'Our people, our villages, our languages, our minds. Have you noticed how we're always scattered? This could be our greatest tragedy. Dreaming of an enlightenment our human minds will never achieve. We try to be smart and progressive, but we really aren't. That is why every philosophy is just that. A philosophy. A utopian concept. An ideology.'

'You're mad, aren't you?' I'm still looking at the well. It is the well that ruined both our lives and here he is, so nonchalant about its existence. I point at it. 'You're telling me I'm being short sighted, because I can't forgive the place my best friend died in? Because you read some whiny philosopher and concluded that this is what enlightenment means?'

'Forget that. Forget everything.'

'Forget the well and live in this house. Right? That's what you were going to say.'

He chuckles. 'We can sit by the river and do some hookah.'

'I don't want your bloody hookah! I want you to shut down that stupid well that killed my best friend and her mother!'

A nerve ticks on his forehead and I think, I've taken it too far. But then, he says to me, 'You don't belong here, Noor. Go home.'

'I *do* belong here. I spent my whole childhood here, of course I belong here.'

He shakes his head, his face a mask. I can tell he looks at me like some metropolis sea urchin who only knows how to talk in designer clothes and Ray Bans. Maybe living in London has changed me, but it has only made me more mature. It hasn't made me uptight or snooty. I'm tired of stereotypes, but once again I will not defend myself. So he goes on, 'My people want plain things. Five finger exercises. Mud under our nails. Retirement at seven in the evening when it gets dark. Pulling carts and making friends. Growing yam and tapioca, and waiting for harvest. Speaking to flowers and interpreting the clouds. Their uncomplicated lifestyle. The fields, the power cuts, the odd beliefs. Their only dreams are to get their little girls married at eighteen, teach their boys ploughing and praying and to have three meals a day, if they can afford it. None of us in this village can even dream about the city and definitely not about London. We have an equation with our calves, our mango trees, our river banks, our soil. We do not understand, and never will, the ways of super structures and high rise buildings. That is all just a delusion for us, Noor. *Maya*. As made up as a chimera.' He looks at me seriously. 'A girl like you will forever be a contrast in a background like that. As long as you don't belong, you just don't. No offense.'

He is watching me intently. There is a multitude of emotions playing on his face and yet I can't read any. It feels like he's known me an entire lifetime. Tears sting my eyes as I turn around. As I'm about to leave I hear him whisper. 'I'm not saying this to hurt you. I'm honestly just looking out for you.'

'Why would you look out for me?'

He doesn't say anything.

My heart flutters as I make a run for it. This is not good. Not good at all. My enslavement to bad things is profound. I don't need to go looking for mistakes, they find me.

It's not been long and already too many bad things have happened.

And I think I've just met the worst of monsters.

Chapter Five

I wake up to damp ceilings and leaking walls. The night brought in a beautiful summer rain and snatched it at the break of dawn. I think about the paintings I've left unfinished back home and how absurd it is that I've actually started missing British tea. And Maggie and her perpetually relaxed face. And how crowded King's Cross was during peak hours yet nobody would push you or cut in front. I've started noticing little things about this place.

People always talk, and most times they don't have nice things to say.

After I'm done freshening up I walk down the stone steps of my front yard to the open fields. I imagine what Maggie would think about all this.

'Blimey, it's so lovely!' she'd say.

I smile to myself. It is indeed.

The wind settles into my hair and I breathe in every memory that has flitted past me today. I am seeing it all now, like a second childhood, I am meeting my best friend in mid-air. I wish it back, what we used to have.

Some things never change. I see her everywhere.

And as I stand there in the field I see my childhood skirt past me like a fast train on an endless track. Kirti and I, we are playing with the marbles again, cheating and stealing and tinkling like temple bells, the sun a spotlight for our childish drama. We are there again, drinking from the lake, trying to touch the fish and put them into our dirty old water bottles. These were our pets, not wolves. We were innocent hearts and we were happy. We were children, lavendered with terror and beauty in a ghost town, and we slept peacefully. We found our friendship in the smallest of joys. Playing tag, climbing trees and chasing ants. We breathed the air of our deities, our homes, and never knew what we were growing into. We were happy.

And then, the memory dissolves into another one. Tell your father to give me my child back, the shopkeeper says, wailing. We are still waiting for our chocolate, but he is gripping Kirti's hand tightly. Her bangles have begun to crack and she's crying out loud. Let go of me! Stop it, let go of me!

Tell your father he will pay for taking Kutta away. Tell him that, little girl. That no matter how many lives we lose and how many you gain, it is your family that will be cursed. He will make sure you fall.

Kirti pulls her hand back. Her bangles are already broken and sticking into her skin. She is tearing up and I hold her, whispering soothing words into her ear. The shopkeeper is agitated and a few villagers have gathered there by now. A man chides, *au onji bale. Budule. She is just a child, leave her. She did nothing wrong.*

But I know what they are all thinking. They are looking at the two of us like we're the spawns of Satan. Like we are bad omens. I pull Kirti towards me and walk away. She is still crying, her eyes red and accusing. We are in the fields again, our feet soggy with mud, stepping on the seeds and the water breaks, and walking back home.

Why are they always doing this to me? She asks tearily. They're always doing this to me and my brother and even my mother. It's not any of our fault. It's his. It's Appa's. And they still always curse us whenever they see us.

I wonder what happened to his son, I say out loud. What did your father do?

She says she doesn't know and it sounds genuine. I put my hand over her shoulder and try to cheer her up.

It's just a bad day, I tell her. Everything is going to be okay.

She sniffs and smiles at me. If only any of us knew. We were condemned by things we had no clue existed.

Suddenly, the grass feels riotous, broader with shamrock, and I feel uneasy. There is a buzz coming out of nowhere and the air is full of dust and sand. I begin to run.

I don't know why, but I feel like something is chasing me. This is not the first time I've felt followed. I know I shouldn't look back, but I do. The minute I turn I trip, and I see red glitter and silver sequin. I am falling, and I lose myself in a rain of sand glitter. I get up again and run with all that I have. This time I don't look back.

I am almost home when I see Arundhati washing clothes on the large stone bench outside her house. When she looks at me she is appalled.

'What did you do?' she asks, and leaving the wet clothes behind, she runs towards me.

'What do you mean?'

She touches my cheek. 'It's red. The whole side, it's red. Like someone slapped you.'

'What?'

'Did you make Rakteswari angry?' she asks me.

I shake my head. I don't understand what she's saying, but somehow she seems to think it's my fault. 'I just want to go in and freshen up. And nobody slapped me, Arundhati. I was in the fields. Maybe I've got an allergic reaction or something.'

She doesn't say anything. Whatever she wants to say is so obviously unbelievable to me that she knows I wouldn't bother heeding her. So she lets it go. But I'm curious about the name she's thrown at me. Rakteswari?

I walk back to Ajja's house. The last thing I want is to be scared away before I get my answers.

*

The next day when Gopi and his wife open the gate to my grandparents' house they are not alone; I see they have brought a guest along and it is the same madcap I've been hoping to never run into for the rest of my stay in Herga. Kohl eyes and the same dicey face. The swelling on my face has gone, but my cheek still hurts. I've no idea what happened, but I've been telling myself it's just allergy. He looks at me strangely, almost as if he can see the tiny marks below my eye. Like little finger nails had dug into my skin. Maybe he knows. Or maybe I'm just reading too much into it. I can think of so many things that have come to his mind and they all worry me. He shouldn't be looking at me like that, nobody should.

I'm half crazy already and my mouth feels so dry. Those basil collars curl around his veiny neck and he's got sleeves rolled up to reveal powerful mocha arms. I stare unabashedly and there's a tiny smirk growing on his lips like he can tell exactly what's cooking in my usually unadulterated head.

'This is Kalki, our village witch doctor. He's been helping us for years now and I told him about the *vetala* in this house,' Gopi says.

'*Jaane?*' I blurt out. *But why?*

Arundhati looks alarmed. 'Noor, you can't live in a place that hasn't been purified. This house has been empty for a long time now. It's not safe. We tried to get help as soon as possible, but Kalki was busy.'

'And you're saying he's going to do something about the so called evil spirits here?'

He's amused by my sarcasm, but remains silent. I

stare at Arundhati, wondering when she'll give me an explanation as to why she's brought him here. After all, hadn't she told me to stay away from their entire family?

'Kalki… is at the top of his game. He's the best we've got. He's stronger than a lot of the spirits here, and honestly, I don't think you need to worry once he performs his rituals.'

'And you think it's safe to have him here?'

Arundhati hesitates. I think she knows Kalki is dangerous, but at the same time she's also very aware of the fact that he may be the only one who can remove the toxic things in this house. And I can't keep denying there's nothing wrong with this place. I've felt stalked ever since I got here.

You might know Kalki...' Arundhati begins again, looking uncomfortable. 'He was...' she looks down and I know she can't bring herself to say it.

'Kirti's brother. Yes, I know.' I extend my hand and Kalki looks at it for a fragment of a second, calculative. He probably finds it funny, but London has taught me that it is wrong to not be polite, even if you're with a stranger. Manners are vital. But maybe this ruffian is never going to understand it.

He finally takes my hand and a flaxen current cuts

into me. Bolts of lighting scatter inside my body and I feel so weak. My heart is suddenly cherry and jam, garnet and merlot pumping into the strongest veins that pattern into my framework like half sewn fabric. I don't know what to do, my hand is limp. And then, he takes his away and I am left standing there like a rag doll. He's still smiling that phony smile and something tells me a cat and mouse chase has only begun. And we all know what happens to the mouse in the end.

I've already started panicking.

He's still standing in the front yard, like a silent predator, as Gopi and his wife take their leave. I don't want them to go, but I can't tell them I'm afraid of this man. They'll laugh at me and remind me that he's here to protect me, not scare me away.

I turn to him grudgingly.

'I've always hated summer.' he tells me. Before I can reply he takes off his shirt. His denim jeans are dangerously low and for some stupid reason my eyes can't look anywhere else. I can't have him parade around here half naked, I just can't. I numb myself to the brooks of tattoos coursing over his taut chocolate skin, his muscles tracing outlines of elm and beech in a cosmos of black snow mountains. This isn't fair to me. He's distracting me from my purpose.

'No,' I reply, annoyed. 'Is this really necessary? And can you put your shirt back on?'

'Why is it bothering you?'

'No,' I lie.

I turn on my heels and try to walk back into the house. He tails me, grabs my arm and turns me around. 'Come on now, don't be such a hothead. We're here for business, nothing else.' He's not smiling anymore, he's serious. I am so aware of his hand resting on my arm and I'm looking right at it. He takes it back and asks, 'Did you see a corpse in the room or did you see something else?'

Startled by the sudden change of topic I stammer. 'He was alive… And I heard him talk.'

'It must have been a *vetala* then. They possess dead bodies. Do you have to stay here? Can't you stay anywhere else? I don't think this place is safe.'

'You think your house is safer?' I ask sarcastically.

'Nowhere in Herga is safe.'

I have so many things to ask him. He's the key to everything I've been seeking, he is my best friend's brother and I just know he knows it all. 'Can you… can you tell me why Kirti died?'

My voice is an air strike, a shuttle raid. It all only boils down to her.

'Never give a sword to a man who can't dance,' he quotes Confucius, the Chinese philosopher. I want to just scream. Where is he going with all of this? He looks at me carefully. And he says, 'What happens if you give a child a sword? He doesn't know what to do with it, he will see power in it, he will not know law or responsibility or nobility. You can't go looking for answers before knowing the roots of this soil. You need to be a part of this system and learn it. Until then, you are an outsider. And, until then, nobody will give you your answers.'

That sounds like a taunt and I can't think of a thing worth saying that will refute him. So I am quiet again, and I let the dull drone of bees moisten the air, wondering if I will ever be able to get what I want out of him. He is not going to make it easy for me, not when he refuses to give me straight answers. How will I get it out of him if he is being so wilful?

'There's nothing you can understand about it unless you understand the culture and beliefs of this village,' he says. 'Unless you start believing everything that you see and hear, you are never going to find out what happened to your childhood friend.'

My eyes light up. So he might tell me after all. 'Will you help me?'

There's a long, difficult silence. He is thinking. And then, he finally says, 'yes.'

His presence overwhelms me. He's not like the rest of us, not when he talks to ghosts so casually. He is an astronomer, an astrologer, Stargazer of the south, spirit caller and shadow priest. He's a sweet talker, a magic wordsmith. I can't endanger myself by rubbing shoulders with him. He is walking fire. And I am the moth that is attracted to flame. I consider packing up and leaving, I can sense that this is going to get out of hand. But then, I remember Kirti, her special smile, the eyes that lit up for the smallest joys, and I forget myself. I want to be brave for her. Even if it means mixing with the wrong crowd.

I am a vacuum of stubbornness. I am here and I will remain here until I get my answers.

After all, he's her brother. How bad can he be?

Chapter Six

And so it begins. We are sitting on the bank of the river, on a slippery boulder. Rivers scare me. They remind me of my people fleeing from attack and jumping into them or their bodies being dumped into them in the aftermath of protests. Suddenly, I'm intrigued by the afterlife. We're scared of the unknown, but what if what's out there is worse than the unknown? I've always believed that we create our own life and death in this world, heaven and hell in sync, but I don't know anymore. I've been speaking to the villagers about Kirti and they tell me nothing but eerie stories.

About how Kirti was always in touch with her mother even after she'd died. That she'd dabbled in the occult and the supernatural to communicate with her. But I don't remember her like that. Ever since aunty had jumped into the well, Kirti had refused to even talk about her. And she hated black magic. She hated that the whole community had isolated her because of her father's profession.

'So do you believe in all of that?' I ask cheekily.

'All of what?' He's making patterns in the water. I could put him on a painting, I think. He's intimidating when he's lost in thought. He is even more beautiful when his face is calm.

'Ghosts. Talking to the dead. I don't know. What do you do? Why is it that the villagers like you so much but never liked your dad?'

His expression changes and he looks bitter. 'My father… wasn't a good man.'

It takes courage to make a confession like that. I don't know what to say. Clouds tempt. Rain is a flirt. A fading rainbow kisses the sky and the horizon is the colour of his hookah smoke. Fireflies are trinkets in the lower sky, ornaments skiing above the waters. There is one on his shoulder, taking asylum. None of these creatures are afraid of him, it is like he is the master of nature.

'He used magic to call spirits, but not out of

possession. He'd help them possess people's bodies. Put curses on families and destroy them.'

Fireflies are a beautiful ribbon around his head. They've settled into his thick curls, and when he darts his piercing charcoal eyes towards me I'm at a loss for words. I want to sit somewhere and pull a sketchbook out, but I know I won't ever do justice to him. You can't put magic so wild on canvas. So, I just watch him watch the river as it plays hide and seek with the stones and wonder what he dreams about when he's asleep. Does he ever think about his family and feel that sinking feeling in his heart? Or is he aloof now, since he's got nothing left to lose?

'Why did he do that?' I ask.

'He had his own clients. Big men with rivalries. They wanted to ruin crops and get rid of the farmers they hated. And then, of course, they wanted my father to channel *yakshis* into bodies of the women who had spurned them. Scorned lovers used to come to our home all the time and ask for help. And he didn't mind as long as they paid him.'

'And you? Do you…' *Do this too?*

'No.'

His face is a silk stream of patience and gentleness. 'He taught me everything he knew, but I use it to…

to get rid of spirits. To protect the people of this place and heal their children. Sometimes it is easier for young kids to be preyed upon. They see things we don't see. And they go into shock and fall sick. I make amulets for them. Or waist bands.'

'And what happens to these spirits you exorcise?'

I don't believe what I'm asking, but I'm still curious. The halo grows stronger, like the fireflies are building home in his hair. I smile a little and he looks up. They're gone now, he's probably wished them away in his head or something. No, that's not humanly possible. I've been cooking up stories and half-baked theories. Maybe I only need some good sleep.

'I nail them into trees. Or trap them in objects that I can bury underground.'

'This is a bit too hard to accept.'

He looks at me like he understands what I mean and holds out his hand. 'I can show you.'

We jump onto the bigger rocks on the shore and finally reach a huge banyan tree. 'Never look up at night, the *yakshis* live there.' He points at a nail hammered into the bark of the tree. It is an old nail and has a rusted spine. 'Put your hand on the nail but don't pull it out. Just put your hand on it.'

I hesitate a little. I don't want to believe it, because it is so illogical, but a part of me is still that village bumpkin who grew up listening to creepy life stories. I look at him and he smiles. He raises his own steel hand and his palm covers mine as I rest it on the nail. 'Close your eyes,' he whispers, and I can feel his breath on my back. I'm not afraid anymore.

'What do you hear?'

'Music.'

A soulful song engulfs my ears and I want to keep listening. I feel seduced, almost pulled into a realm I cannot explain. The only thing that could come close to this is sirens luring sailors and causing shipwrecks. The music is so ethereal, I start seeing things. A woman with a child, jumping into a pyre. A flashback of a dancer in a palace. Courtesans cheering and throwing flowers at her feet. And then, the scene dissolves into another. A little girl sold into slavery. Locked inside walls. It's all flashing in front of me like a supercut, and the music grows louder. I'm hallucinating now and I don't want to open my eyes.

'Noor.' My name on his lips sounds like heaven. A landslide of melodies. I'm feverish now and I can feel his grip tighten on my hand as he pulls it back. His hand is on my waist and moving upwards. He pulls me back and I fall on him. We are both on the ground, holding onto each other.

My eyes flutter open. 'What was that?'

He's laughing now. 'I don't know. You tell me.'

I don't want to talk about what happened after I stopped listening to the tree song. That is lethal to my system. So I go back to what I experienced.

'Was that a ghost talking to me?'

He widens his eyes mockingly. 'A ghost? Well, Noor. I thought ghosts didn't exist.' He mimicks my voice and I lurch at him, laughing.

'Listen,' I say. 'I want to know what that was. Or else, I'm going to assume you put thoughts in my head.'

He leans against the bark of the tree. 'Thoughts? What kind of thoughts would I put in your head?' Suddenly, the air is thicker. There is too much chemistry between us to ignore, but I will fight it to the last bone. This is a boy who probably grew up on riverbanks, singing to mermaids and water nymphs. I wouldn't last a day if I fell for him.

And I know that it would kill my mother if she knew who I was associating with. She'd grown up in Herga and knew Krishna uncle very well. In the sense that he'd always been trouble and so had his family.

They let me play with Kirti but always forbade me from staying in her house after dark. My mother once told me that it was because Krishna uncle would send a ghost after me if the sun set.

But I thought these were stories told to frighten kids, not adults.

Then why am I feeling so scared now?

'What did I hear inside that tree?' I ask him, dubious.

'There's a *yakshi* trapped in there. She was just trying to lure you into pulling out the nail.'

'She sings like a siren.'

'Looks like one too.'

There's silence exploding like confetti in the air. I can hear distant cows and children laughing. 'Are they really beautiful?'

He chuckles. 'Why?'

I shake my head. 'Never mind.' I begin to walk away from him. 'I'm going home.'

'It's not even midday.'

'I don't want to be hanging out with you if we are spending any more time not finding answers.'

'But you always spent time with my sister.'

'That's different!'

He shrugs. 'The only difference is that she was a girl. I don't know what other difference you see.'

'Well, for one,' I say in defence. 'She never played around with all this sorcery and shit. And she was always polite and sweet.'

He blinks. 'I can be sweet too.'

'And she never wore kajal.'

'You wore it. All the time.'

I'm tired of him telling me how well he observed me. Either he is a very observant person or he'd just picked me out in a crowd, or both. I don't want to ask him how he knew all of this. He'd seen me around here and there, but only from afar. How could someone take note of so many things?

'That's not the point,' I say. 'Only girls wear kajal. When boys wear it, it's…' *girly*, I want to tell him. Feminine. But no amount of convincing myself is going to go against living proof that he doesn't look feminine at all. In fact the kajal makes him look hot. But of course I don't want him to know that.

'And then, again, if boys wanted to wear kajal, they should.' I didn't know what point I was trying to make. I realized I was the one being an uneducated hillbilly here, so I shut my mouth. It's okay, I tell myself, feeling guilty. Sometimes conditioning can do that to you. It doesn't mean you should call your mother a little less.

'It's okay. You're not your mother. You're Noor Haque, a person of your own,' he tells me, and I'm taken aback. He couldn't have read my thoughts, could he?

'What *are* you?' I ask him, taking a step back.

'Perhaps the Übermensch.'

I look confused. 'And what is that?'

'Noor. You're so smart and you're telling me you don't know what that is?' he jokes.

Suddenly, I'm on guard and I cross my arms. 'Well, I don't know, so tell me.'

'Have you heard of Nietzsche?'

I nod. I have no idea how he knows so much. I'm going to steal all his books one day from that secret library of his. That's the only way I can even dream of holding an argument with him.

'It's just a concept in his philosophy. He wrote a book, *Thus Spoke Zarathustra*, where he talks about this. It means superman or overman or whatever you'd like to call it. It represents a higher biological type reached through artificial selection. Someone who has mastered the whole of human potential.'

I scoff. 'And you think you're this… this overman?'

He laughs like I've cracked a joke. 'You asked me what I was and I wanted to give you a believable answer. I talk to ghosts, I tame wolves and read palms. I join stars and horoscopes. Maybe I know a lot more than the average human does.'

'Or maybe you're just a pompous ass.'

He laughs it off and says, 'Maybe.'

But now that I've heard ghosts sing and the villagers tell me about all that their local black magician has done, I don't know what to believe anymore. I know that the last thing I should do is trust him, but I've bought into every word he's ever said, and I don't know if it's these words that terrify me or if that mouth does.

I have never felt so possessed by someone until now. He has taken over my thoughts and something tells me he will soon take over my heart too.

I need to find my answers fast, before I sink.

*

In the evening I sit in Ajja's veranda and sip coffee. I've been wandering around the old house looking at Ajja and Ajji's black and white photos. I don't know much about my history, apart from the fact that my maternal family lived here, and so did I, for a long while. I wonder if I'll ever be a true Kashmiri, because I know I'll always run back to my mother's place. There's too much nostalgia hitting me blind these days and I feel sick.

Every time I text my parents I feel guilty, like I'm doing something wrong. It's not the running away bit, that's probably expected of a free spirit like me, but this is taking it too far. I've been spending time with the most notorious person in Herga. I'd be skinned alive if they knew the kind of company I was keeping.

When are you coming back? – Baba

Maybe I should call him.

'Baba?'

The voice on the other end is feeble. I want to ask him how he is, but I already know that with everything going on he isn't too well.

'Noor, *beta*. How long are you going to stay there in that makeshift excuse for a house? What if the roof falls? Have you called help or something?'

'Baba, I need to be here a few more days. I just want closure with Kirti. To know why she did what she did.'

There is a long pause on the other end, and then, he says, 'Sometimes, some things in life can't be answered, my child. You need to come back some time.'

'I will. What's the situation in Kashmir?' I ask, bracing myself for the news.

'I hear they're going to impose curfew in all ten districts.'

'Curfew?'

'Yes. Mobile services will be suspended. Something else happened in Srinagar a few days back. Naeem Akhtar's residence was attacked with petrol bombs.'

'What! Is he dead?'

'No, no. He wasn't there at that time. Neither was his family.'

'This is crazy!'

'I know, I know. I was thinking, maybe I shouldn't rush you into coming back. I mean it's okay if you want to, but…'

I can tell he's worried. If he could help it he'd send me back to London. But he knows that I'm stubborn. I'm not going back until I find out what's happened.

'I'll stay here longer, Baba. Don't worry.'

'Don't get into trouble. We all know that place is no good. And forget Kirti, Noor. I know it's difficult, but you know their family had a reputation. She was a good girl and… I don't believe in all this curse nonsense, but still. I don't know, *beta*. It's just better for us not to go poking our noses into things not meant for us.'

'Okay, Baba.'

*

A lone wolf howls in wisps of an echo. I go back in and look out through my window. I see him there, oceans away from me, looking back. His silhouette is like a silent battleship, slipping into the oblivious night. For as long as eternity he stands there and waits for me to leave. I pull one curtain towards me and peep through it. The light switches off and he is gone.

He is a half dream anyway. He could be imaginary for all I know.

And then, I see him walk out of the house and towards the well. My heart skips a beat as he stands there, pondering. What is he doing? Is he going to jump? Now I see it. All the wolves encircling him as he sits down against the stone walls of the well. There is a woman beside him. I can tell by her long, curly hair and flowing red *sari*. I can't see her face, but she has the most glistening complexion.

They don't even seem to acknowledge each other. Godless, they smoke hookah, sitting on their own sides.

Chapter Seven

It's the third week of August and Baba tells me that people are being hit by teargas shells. Pro-freedom rallies are being held at Anantnag, Shopian and Pulwama. Security forces are constantly trying to disperse people, but there is a lot of unrest. They are also getting injured. I feel homesick all of a sudden. I want to be there with my family when there is so much happening.

'Who was she?' I ask him when he comes to my doorstep.

We are going to watch a special show, he says. Herga hosts the best *yakshagaana*.

'Who?'

'The woman in red?'

'I don't know what you're taking about.'

He does. He's stiffened.

'Fine,' I huff. 'Don't tell me anything. You can't fool me. I saw her with my own eyes.'

He doesn't look at me. 'Sometimes it is better to not believe your own eyes. Sometimes being stupid is being smart. Or at least pretending to be.'

'So you're saying I should act like I never saw her?'

'Saw who?' He smiles.

I put my hands up. 'Okay, okay. I get it.'

'You've got a long life, Noor. Don't waste it on silly questions.'

I put my hands on my hips and face him. 'How do you know if I've got a long life?'

He chortles, 'Always so inquisitive. I can predict the future. I'm psychic.'

'Yeah, right,' I roll my eyes.

'No, really. Here, give me your hand.'

'You're asking for my hand?' I hold back a smile.

'Not that way, silly. But just give me your hand, please?'

'Why?'

'I'll show you.'

I put my hand out, palm facing him. He traces it lightly with his finger, 'See this? This is the lifeline.'

'Ooh, scary.'

He is reading my palm, but I am so fascinated by his hands. They're like static electricity, it's like the minute they touch me I'm on fire. What are you doing to me, you wolf child? My mind taunts and I try to suppress it. If I am a little louder he might just hear me, and that is the last thing I want.

I think I could be falling for him and this is depressing me. I don't even know him and I'm so nonplussed by the kind of feelings orbiting my head. What do I even want?

Nevermind that, I know exactly what I want.

Only the things that I can't have.

If ever Amma gets to know that I've been having feelings for someone like him...

To Amma, he and his family have always been vermin. The worst of riff-raff. To a Brahmin there was no caste higher than theirs, and it would have been funny if it hadn't been so serious, because it wasn't as if we had a say in castes. My mother married outside of her religion. Hell, she married a Muslim man! She ran away from home and came back to her parents only after she'd had a baby. I'm only half a Brahmin, but apparently that still meant everything. I was still royalty, even though it made no difference to me. They made sure it did. They made sure I was aware of how superior I was.

I remember my grandparents taking me to a Hindu temple when I was a little girl. Was it the Krishna Math? I watched the Dalits roll over the leftover food Brahmins had eaten over plantain leaves.

'Why're they dirtying themselves, Ajja?'

'They're purifying themselves. It rids them of bad karma. It's called *Madey Snana*, a bath in leftovers.'

Ever since, I have been embarrassed of where I came from. I was scared they'd say something insulting to Kirti. Bringing her home meant introducing her to my family and I was scared they would hurt her. But if I didn't invite her home she would think I was embarrassed of her. It was a complicated situation. So I put that at the back of my mind and loved her fiercely. It was all that I could do.

They never let Kirti come home much and they definitely didn't let her stay over for sleepovers. The only sleepovers we'd had were when I'd sneak out to go to her place. My parents used to keep pulling me away from her, but I'd find ways to be with her.

She is not good for you, Amma would try to explain. 'She's a good girl and we like her a lot, but her family is harmful. She might be naïve now, but she's going to grow up and become one of them.'

Do not step into that house, it is full of evil, Ajji would say. And even Ajja would look upon them in distaste, claiming that that family has always put the whole village in trouble.

And now, here I was, with someone they feared even more than a girl as innocent and childish as Kirti. Her black magician of a brother. Touching me. Holding my palm towards him, reading it out loud with that sinfully provocative mouth of his...

Stop it, Noor, my head rings. I've got one foot in reality and the other in dreams. And if I don't curb these dreams I'll end up in the hottest circles of hell.

But I can't deny it, I've been thinking about him a lot.

'You've got a very long life,' he says, a twinkle in his eyes. 'And you're going to have the time of your life in your... twenties... around the time you're... twenty-five?' he asks. I nod.

'So that's now,' I drone.

'That's now,' he grins. 'And apparently, it's because you'll meet a very charming young man who's going to show you around one of the most notorious villages...'

By then, I'm yanking my hand back and rolling over in laughter. 'Please!'

He looks offended. 'What? You don't believe me?'

I roll my eyes. 'No, no. Of course I believe you!'

We're bantering by the time we reach our destination, and it's a good kind of banter. Light hearted. Like candyfloss. Melting inside mouths. Tasting of saccharine. Spreading sweetness all over your insides with the slightest of bitter aftertaste. Steaming up like a Turkish bath. Gummed to the tummy with butterflies. The three winged kind. The colour of unicorn and feathers. The best kind, when one doesn't have to define this banter. When one doesn't have to put a name to this friendship or whatever it is.

You'd love the libraries in England, I tell him. I wish I could bring them to you.

He's all smiles. 'You're the sweetest thing, Noor. But all that is just not for me.'

'No, really. For someone who reads as much as you do, I can imagine how wonderful it would feel.

Who is your favourite writer?'

His answer is immediate. 'Bukowski. Dostoyevsky. Maybe Margaret Atwood.'

I'm riveted now. 'You like Margaret Atwood? What do you like?'

'I really liked The Handmaid's Tale.'

'Hmm.' I am smiling now. At last we have similar interests. No more Chinese philosophers and women bashing writers. He has been swayed by a feminist. 'Do you think that'll happen to women? Will we lose control over our bodies one day? It's possible, isn't it?'

I expect him to burst out laughing, but he is only smiling at me adorably. I want to tell him to stop, that it's making my insides feel so light.

'Anything is possible,' he says. 'Not just to women, but to all of mankind. We are a dying race.'

'Oh, come on. Don't say that. That's very pessimistic.'

'We have already lost control of our minds. How long before we lose control over our bodies too?'

'I liked The Handmaid's Tale. It was very insightful.'

'Yes, it was,' he says, and there it ends.

Yes, it was, I think. I don't know what to say next, but for the first time I'm not panicking for the lack of conversation. I'm comfortable sharing words with him, and even more comfortable sharing silence with him.

I look at him, striding by my side towards nowhere, and accept that maybe it's okay to fall. Why not, if the falling is this easy? Or maybe he's just playing some ridiculous magic trick on me, who knows.

All at once, there are fireflies around us again. I look up. This time I'm the one with the halo.

He turns to me and smiles.

*

Twilight meanders into the air as we sit on the plastic chairs the organizers have arranged for us. There aren't many people here except for a few school kids and the two of us. I rest my head on his shoulder, testing him, but he doesn't move. My mouth is dry, filled with the loss of unsaid words, but I can't believe I'm watching a native performance and that this is my first real date with him. In London, I would have been asked out for a nice movie. We'd have hot chocolate and marshmallows by the fireplace. But this is not London, this is Herga, and we are watching a splendid *yakshagaana*, and today I wouldn't have wanted to watch this with anyone else.

I'm so greedy for this moment, I can't imagine sharing it with anyone else, not even Kirti.

The musicians begin to sing in unison. Bold, clear goldenrod and canary. I taste bitter lemon and sun glow at the base of my throat, I feel like singing and rejoicing with them. Why does everything in this village provoke my emotions so well? I look at him from the corner of my eye. This is a man who belongs to the night. Moonlight devours his face with its splash. Light touches upon his cheek like a sable paintbrush focusing on detail. I see the kohl clearly. It is smudged and smoky. I am so fascinated I just want to touch him. Man of wolves. And I still do not know who he is.

The *yakshagaana* goes on for some time. The *pungi*, *maddale* and *harmonium* float on the most enriching of *ragas*. My heart is honeyed. I have never listened to anything so lovely. The drums bring the *Tenkutittu* actors to life. I have never seen so much sincerity and unity in song and dance.

'I like this,' I exclaim. 'All the dance forms and folk art I've seen are always related to some story in a religious text.' I shrug. 'It's all so beautiful, but I wish people were a little less fanatic about it. It feels like indoctrination at times.'

And, yet again, I'm curious to know what he thinks about all this. So I ask, 'Do you believe in it?'

He shakes his head.

Do you not follow any religion then? I ask him again.

I was labeled a Hindu, he admits grudgingly.

'But you're not?'

'I don't think I'm one for religions,' he comments. 'I don't know about god, but religion sucks the life out of people. All these great books that we've written in the name of religion, the Bible, the Ramayana, whatever. Do they teach us feminism? Do they teach us empathy? Respect towards each other? Where was feminism when Draupadi was disrobed or Sita was banished for no fault of hers? Where was feminism when Eve was being blamed for everything gone wrong in Eden? Where was justice when Persephone was abducted or when the Bible doles out instructions for slave masters and condemns homosexuality? Or maybe it doesn't. Maybe I'm wrong and maybe we've all interpreted it wrong. But there is no point holding up a religious text as holy when none of its tenets are being followed. It's all pretty on paper. By the end of the day what matters is how well humans have imbibed goodness into them. It doesn't matter how great the book is. It doesn't matter if you pray everyday. It only matters if you lived a life that was meaningful to you and to others. We all know what religion does to us. We're so fanatic about our gods that we forget to think about our people. We kill each other and say our gods made us do it. It is our hands, isn't it? We're carrying it a bit too far. It's getting to our heads and we are forgetting to be what God made us, if ever there is a god. We're forgetting to be human.'

'And what about all of this? What do you think?' I ask again, waving my hand at the little kids wearing *bhoota* masks and dancing around with lanterns. I want someone to just tell me that they don't believe in the dark side, in the supernatural, or even that they do, just give me a fixed answer. I'm so bewildered, caught in wishful thinking, frail and injected by faith. I need a yes or a no, and I need a reason why. I'm tired of hearing and seeing things but never being able to completely believe anything. My mind is always on crossroads, but just a step closer to logical reasoning.

'In *yakshagaana*?'

'In ghosts… in the stories they weave for these dramas. I don't know.' I wave my hand carelessly. 'In the supernatural.'

'I don't know anymore, what to believe or not believe in.'

'There are a lot of things about this place I'd like to not believe in,' I add.

He grins. Then he's suddenly grave again. 'There

are a lot of things I'd like to believe in. But above all, I'd just like to believe in myself.'

Me too, I want to admit. But I don't know. I am in love with his thoughts. I don't want to interrupt him and I don't want to interfere in whatever world he is losing himself in. It is of the most beautiful solitude. I could never pull it off. I can never draw the line between solitude and loneliness, somewhere they merge and become one.

I wonder if he ever feels the same way.

'What after this?' I whisper into his ear, and he looks at me smilingly.

'Did you like it?'

'I loved it. I'm slowly starting to understand the culture. It's a celebration of life and death. I don't think the villagers are still used to me, but at least they're kind.'

'They'll come around, don't worry.'

I like the sound of him when he's reassuring, but I don't tell him that. After another long silence, he says, 'I'm going to show you something you will never forget next. It's called a *kola*.'

'What's that?'

'Kind of like a possession.'

'What?!'

'It's not scary, don't worry.' He laughs at my expression. 'Nobody is going to die. Well, I hope.'

'Aren't you afraid of death?' I ask him.

'There are worse things than death,' he replies calmly.

'Oh? Like what?'

'Losing someone you love,' he says.

I'm shut again. Sometimes he says such heart breaking things, it leaves me lost. 'Kalki…' I begin, but he interrupts me.

'Shh. This is the main part. Watch.' He diverts his attention to the stage again and I watch his expression change. It's alert, full of interest and awe, and I'm more captivated by this personal show than what's on stage.

I wonder what's happening to me. This is more magic than I can handle.

*

At ten we move towards a garden of tents. There is a big bonfire in the middle and a couple of men holding onto someone with a mask.

'This is a *kola*. That person is possessed by the village spirit.'

'These *bhootas* are guardians of the village, of the Tulu tribes settled here. To appease and solicit assistance from the spirits, the villagers conduct this ceremony,' he tells me.

'Why are they holding onto him?'

'Because he might harm himself.'

The man is dancing and wriggling and running towards the bonfire. I'm scared he might just jump, but the men are strong enough to hold him down. As I look into the eyes of the man who is performing the *kola*, I see death. They're sunken and lifeless, and yet there's a wild dance boiling inside them. The tension in the air is eery and I move closer to Kalki. I know that if I stay here any longer it'll ruin me. I turn to Kalki and I read the same expression on his face. He knows exactly what I'm thinking and he's fearing the same thing. This is too much to see in one sitting.

'Do you want to leave?' he asks me, concerned.

I shake my head. All at once my curiosity has become an Achilles heel.

When we take our seats on the wet grass, the performer grabs a chicken passing him and bites into it. He gobbles it up raw and there is blood everywhere. I look away, and the minute I do Kalki's hand shoots up and covers my face. His palm is resting lightly on my cheek and he's pulling me towards his shoulder.

I freeze. I'm terrified when boys are nice to me. It means I'm in trouble. It always means I'm in trouble. But now there are worse things to fear, so I let him touch me, I let him support my head and protect me.

I close my eyes and sob into his shirt. I'm so scared of this. Living in a state of war back home was difficult enough. I don't know which monsters are scarier. The human demons that we know or the unknown ghosts that haunt us. I can't live like this. And he knows it too.

I've slowly started believing the village's horror stories.

Chapter Eight

Apparently a body was found in the Jhelum river today. They've imposed curfew in Srinagar, Badgam, Ganderbal, Bandipora and Handwara. In the village of Zangalpora, Kulgam, protestors set a policeman's house on fire. Again in Kulgam, a Jawahar Navodaya Vidyalaya caught fire.

I can't imagine how my parents are feeling right now. I know they must be scared and I feel terrible for not being there with them during this crisis. But they'll never let me come back at such a terrible time. They wouldn't want me to take the risk.

For now even Herga is safer than Kashmir, they'd say.

*

Last night I had the most uncanny of experiences. I couldn't sleep properly, I kept seeing the *bhoota kola* in my nightmares and I kept waking up at odd times. I kept hearing the little boy *vetala* crying and laughing and falling out, lifeless. I think I'm going crazy. A part of me tells me that all my problems stem from just one person and the solution to all of this is simple. Leave the company of the black magician and do my own research. But how will I ever find out what happened to Kirti if I don't talk to Kalki?

If Kirti was out of this equation would you still talk to Kalki? My mind taunts me and I inspire no answers.

I try not to think of him. I don't even know him and here I am, running around with him. I can tell the villagers have already started talking about us spending time together. I wonder if they like us together or if they think it's absurd.

Because I quite like the idea of us.

I shake myself out of these silly thoughts. I can't afford to be like this. If Ajja and Ajji had been around they'd have shot me dead.

I don't know what I'm doing. My upbringing tells me I'm supposed to feel dirty about all this, but I've never felt so clean and pure. I'm letting my ancestors down. I'm bringing dogs home as Amma would put it.

But I think of his *shisha* mouth and I unhinge. I'm so distracted already. It's ridiculous, but the thought of him soothes me, and yet unsettles me. I think of brown. Bridges and landslides of espresso. Oak and acorn spread over pastures of metal shine. Meadows of pinecone. Sweep of tree rings. He is a Tasmanian tiger, a gust of the feral wind. And his eyes, they take over me like nothing has. They're sweet talkers, verses anchored in a quiet domain.

The house is so empty and I feel so lonely. Solitude chars me. I'm black soot when I'm alone and my imagination runs to the devil's workshop. I feel like an outcast in this village of power cuts and tribal ghost stories and my only friends are my Ajja's servants and the wonder boy with the voodoo fingers.

Fingers that go on and on like train tracks. I feel goosebumps flare up on melanin and I close my eyes. *Stop it, Noor. Shut these thoughts out. You don't need them now. You are here to find answers to Kriti's death, you cannot let yourself stray.*

But as it is, I am drawn to things not meant for me. So I put on my shawl, tie my hair up and set out to his house.

I already see him from a distance, sitting in the veranda with a book in his hand. He is smoking and he is thinking. These are the two things he does most. Smoke and think. I wonder what the point is, thinking so much, reading and educating himself so much, and yet constraining himself to this dull land of rurals. Why can't he leave and make a good living? He is one of the smartest people I know.

It takes courage to be a man of simple words. And yet, there's something holding him back. What's left for him here? Why can't he move out and do something about his life instead of just smoking and reading?

A boy like that doesn't belong in the city, my grandmother would say. But a boy like that doesn't belong in the village either, not when he's so gifted. I think about Kalki in London, in a dashing suit, leading board meetings and traveling the world. I think about him in Ralph Lauren, lying in a five star hotel room preparing for his next talk on Murakami and Marx and god knows who. So what is he doing here? Does he even have anyone to talk to?

I feel like I am his first real friend in a world of monsters, and I am grateful that we met. He is their God, because he saves them from their greatest fears. But if someone asked me I'd say it is his humanity that makes him God. Kalki is shamelessly, bravely human. Nothing else. It is empathy, the need to help others, that makes us all gods. It is our cruelty that makes us monsters.

'Look who's here,' he drawls, and I already feel like I'm in trouble. It's even more disconcerting to know that this is exciting me. I take a few steps further. Unhooked moments and untied smiles. I feel like a fighter kite all of a sudden, being played into a war I never wanted to be a part of.

'What brings you here? Not me, of course.' He rises from his easy chair and walks towards me.

No, not you. I want to say, but I'm bad at lies. I should have thought of a good cover up before running out impulsively. What am I thinking, god.

'I was just taking a walk to the family temple.'

He raises his eyebrow. There is a laugh playing on his lips, but he's trying his best to hide it and wear a serious face. 'The temple is that way,' he says, pointing to the opposite direction.

'Oh. I guess I…got confused.'

'Right.'

I've run out of things to say. So I ask him abruptly, 'Why are you always reading?'

His response is straightforward. 'Because it makes me happy.'

I think about all the drawing room talks and coffee table debates I've had in England. There is so much opportunity to provoke thought and I feel so sad that nobody will ever get to know his mind.

He is an inmate in this village of phantasms.

'What are you reading now?'

He holds up the book so that I can read the cover. 'The Myth of Sisyphus.'

'He's you and me, no doubt.' He puts the book aside. 'And all the rest of us.'

I don't want to ask what that's supposed to mean, so I let the silence linger. He can tell me if he wants to. Or not.

'Why are you here?' he asks me. 'Tell me honestly.'

'Just like that,' I deflect. 'I don't need a reason to go for a walk.'

'Why do you do that? Why do you always keep such a big distance when you talk? Not physically. But emotionally, you're always so distant. Or you try to make yourself so. Did someone hurt you before?' he says.

For a long while I'm unable to speak. Then he takes my name and there are butterflies coursing through every nerve under my skin. 'Noor?'

'No,' I say, thinking, trying to find the right words. I need to make this as clear as possible. 'It's just been like that. I can't be too friendly. Maybe it's just my nature, or maybe it's something I have acquired over the years from everything I have experienced. I don't open up easily, and in a modern society where hook-up culture is what's trendy, I forget myself. Nobody wants to take time to sit over a cup of iced tea and talk about stars, places and people. Nobody wants to know your name or the way you pronounce it, or the number of languages you can write it in. Nobody wants to talk about the lullabies our grandmothers sang us or the bed time stories our grandfathers told us or even which stars we'd like to sleep under and whether we're a moon or sun person, whether we stay up late or wake up early, if we like our coffee black, if we like old Disney movies and spaceships. Hell, I don't know.' I take a deep breath. I know I'm all over the place, dissociating from myself, but I don't care anymore. I need to get this out. 'What I'm trying to say is, nobody wants to take the time to get to know each other. Nobody cares. Nobody wants minds, it's too much to take. They just want bodies, they want to get it over with. So I shut myself. I want them to know I'm difficult, because I am. Because first impressions aren't always real impressions. Everything is layered with a big fat sugar coating, we're all trying to impress each other, faking how smart we are, trying to show off, trying to look the best, the prettiest, the nicest. But the truth about us humans is that we can't stay polite too long. Anger is a real emotion. Love is real. Pain is real. But we all want to switch it off and pretend to be so plastic, it's not even funny.'

He's intrigued, empathetic, knowing. His eyes, they're full of questions, full of things to tell. He looks like he's got all the right answers for what I've said, but there is also a time to reveal them. So he says, 'I agree. Love is real.'

Suddenly, I'm so aware that it's just the two of us there. I look away, wondering how I got here at all.

'So did you enjoy last night's show?' he asks. I welcome the change of topic.

I nod. 'Yes. Except the chicken eating bit. I don't think I really… er… enjoyed that.'

'It's common. They eat chickens, eat fire, do all sorts of nonsense.'

'Don't you think it's real?'

He looks up. 'I don't see how *bhoota kolas* can be performed all the time, in everyone's house, the minute someone asks for it. You can't choose to get possessed.'

'But you *do* believe in the supernatural,' I stress.

'Don't you? After all that you've seen?'

I look away and he goes on. 'Too much has happened for me to not believe.'

Just like Gopi's wife, Arundhati, I do not know what superstition is anymore. They say superstition claws its way out of uneducated minds. But what if the logical believe in them too? Are they superstitions then or are they parts of the utmost terrifying reality?

Or maybe all of us, just all of us might be losing our minds.

'Can I come in?' I ask.

He turns around and I can tell he's not sure. Something is up. His house looks like there are people inside. Or rather, a person. Curious I walk towards the house and he follows me. 'I didn't invite you in.'

'It's my best friend's house, I used to barge in whenever I wanted.'

'You're going to regret this,' he says, running after me and grabbing my hand.

'Let go, it's Kirti's house! I'm invited all the time!'

'Kirti is *dead*, Noor.' Both of us stop in our tracks. 'She jumped into the same well my mother jumped into. She hit her head on one of the rocks and bled or drowned to death. You,' he says, pointing at me, his hands shaking with cold rage, 'need to just stop talking about her in present tense.'

I tear up. He doesn't know what to do. Both of us just stand there and my tears don't stop. I miss her so much and I can tell he misses her even more. But she is gone and the only thing we can do is try to move on.

'Okay, fine. Come in. But just don't touch anything or even say anything.'

'Why, what's going on in there?'

'You'll see.'

When I enter the living room I see a woman in a bright red sari sitting there.

My heart stills. It's her. The woman I saw the other night, the very same woman who had been smoking with him. She's absolutely gorgeous, arresting even. She watches me with a small smile, one finger on her crooked lips. Calculative. There are glass bangles on her wrist and a big bindi on her forehead. I want to say something to him, but Kalki doesn't even look at her. He walks into one of the other rooms and I allow my feet to take me after him. There is no conversation anywhere, no sound, except the gentle sobbing of a woman coming from the room we have entered into.

I never knew this house was so big. Of course it should be. It is an ancestral house. All the black magicians of this village have lived here. It is wide and spacious, but very old. It looks like it will fall apart any time.

But Kalki doesn't seem so bothered about it. Maybe it is magic that is holding the house together like a pack of cards. Maybe it is the family ghost. But what am I saying. Ghost?

It's better not to think about any of these things. I'd like to stay sane a bit longer than the rest of them.

The wailing grows louder and that's when I see her. Crouched on the floor, biting into her own hand and screaming. A young woman, delirious to the point of insanity. She is in pain and blood drips from her arm like leaves falling in autumn. Her kajal smudged eyes look deranged and I grab onto Kalki's arm. He looks at me from the corner of his eyes, and then, whispers, 'Don't worry. She's not possessed. She's just very scared.'

His wolves are sitting next to her, alert. Suddenly, she jerks and makes a dash for the door. Before she can even reach it the wolves block her path, but they don't growl. They don't threaten her. They are compassionate towards her, they don't want to scare her. She is not the abuser, she is the victim.

Kalki walks towards her and hands her a pendant. She's already got four of them around her neck, I'm led to believe that a ritual was going on even before I got here. She begins to cry. 'You won't see them again. Don't take this off until I tell you to,' he says.

She's made to wait another fifteen minutes as Kalki returns to the verandah and takes a drag. When he gets back inside the house there's another pendant hanging from his pocket. 'This is the last one. Wear it. We'll see for a week. If it works you can take them off.'

She thanks him, fresh tears springing from her eyes. As she leaves the house the woman in red follows her out. It is almost as if she is making sure she's safe all the way back to her house. She puts her palms together as she faces Kalki and he does the same. By the time he bolts the door I am perplexed beyond explanation.

'What the hell was that?'

'I told you not to come in.'

'No, it's not that I regret it. I just want to know what happened.'

He takes a deep breath. 'That girl you just saw? She's been having nightmares. Seeing things. She skipped all her exams, tried to burn her clothes. Her mother claims she hasn't slept a wink and that she's always crying. She's lost a lot of weight and barely talks to anyone anymore.'

'Maybe she's depressed,' I suggest. I worked with the British National Health Service for a few years in Nottingham so I can tell from these signs, she's definitely suffering from mental illness. Anybody can tell, in fact. It just seems that obvious. I want to tell him that she was having hallucinations, but I know he has a different theory for all of this.

'She took out a nail from a tree. Since then, it's been after her,' he responds quietly.

'What's been after her?' I ask.

He doesn't answer and I'm left in the dark again.

Chapter Nine

There is an outbreak of war in Kashmir and I am running, my suitcases in hand, but I don't know where I'm going. It is Herga again, and I see corrals of trees, their branches looking like outstretched arms. Don't look up, I tell myself. I am running again and my feet carry me to no destination. Everywhere I turn is a dead end. I want to go back to London, but my heart isn't there anymore. My heart is a land of the dead.

'Kalki!' I scream. 'Baba! Amma! Daadi! Help!'

Akka, akka. Chooru enne kolera. Please give me some oil.

It is raining oil and there is high pitched laughter. The wolves howl, but they're nowhere to be seen.

Krishna uncle watches me from the old house. He is holding Kirti prisoner and she's begging me to run.

'Don't get involved in this, Noor,' she says. 'I'm sorry I dragged you into this.'

'Kalki!' I scream. Kalki, Kalki, Kalki.

Vetala. *Something whispers back.*

My cheeks are wet. Help me, I whisper into the night, and the darkness engulfs me like a black curtain.

I wake up in a pool of sweat. I'm shivering and I rub my forehead vigorously. I can't do this anymore, I think. I can't stay here. Why am I having so many bad dreams? And who am I dreaming about, of all people? Angered and embarrassed I reach out for my phone. I need to know if my family is safe. And I need to not tell them about my new dirty secret.

I hope they won't catch me in my lie. *Yes, Baba, I am fine. No, Baba, there is nobody in Kirti's house and I haven't been going there.*

Have I found out why Kirti did what she did? No, I haven't.

I've been… distracted.

But Baba hasn't called in days. He hasn't texted either.

I'm worried now, there is so much happening in Kashmir and I'll never know what my family is up to unless I hear from them directly. I feel like the weather. Stormy.

*

I try to get a newspaper from the nearest shop and some sleeping pills. I haven't been sleeping properly. I'm always waking up at odd hours, and for the first time in my life I'm scared of living in Ajja's house. I dream of the boy and his face transforms into someone else who then becomes the one man I should really be afraid of. Everything finds its way to him. When I see hookah for sale in shops, or philosophy books, or even when I see tarot cards, I am reminded of him.

I don't know what spells he's been using on me.

On my way back I rent a bicycle. It is easier to travel these timeless streets on a bike, because the travel is so long and it gets dark quickly. And once it is dark there is nobody on the road.

I leave another text for Baba and try ringing him up. The last I spoke to Amma she told me to visit the family temple. Most families in Herga have a demon, a ghost, a god, or whatever it is that we call *bhoota*, who protects us. We build small temples near our homes for this *bhoota*, who brings good luck to the family and wards off evil. I want to tell Amma about the incident with the *vetala* in Ajja's house, but I don't want her to worry. She's spent her whole life running away from her family and its traditions. It's weird that she's suddenly asked me to go to the temple. Maybe, deep down, she really is scared that I'm living here alone.

But I'm twenty-five and I get to be wherever I want without asking anyone's permission.

The temple looks worn out and untended. It's been years since Ajji set her foot here. When she was alive she used to come here every morning and pray. Now nobody comes and the walls have been eaten up by moss.

There is a lone idol in the middle of the temple, and as I walk towards it I can feel that I'm not alone.

Maybe I'm just imagining it. Sometimes when you hear too many stories you start making up your own. That's how peculiar the human mind is. That's just how complex it is.

As I move closer I begin to hear things.

Growls.

It's one of his wolves again, I think. Or rather, I hope. But I know his wolves don't growl like that. It's singing to me from behind the stone idols. I'm tempted to run, but I need to calm my mind down and be a little rational. A part of me says that by looking and confirming it is nothing I'll feel better. A part of me says that by looking it'll no longer be the unknown and I'll no longer be scared.

And then, I see it. It is her again, and there is something on her lap with its intestines torn open. The girl who'd been chewing her arm in Kalki's house. All the pendants are shattered on the ground and she is looking at me like she could eat me. Her open palms, red. Wine spilling all over her shawl, the colour of sunset. She is still growling as she bends down to bite into whatever she has hunted. My skin is sick with goosebumps. I cannot move. I want to look away, but my eyes are screaming, stuck in their sockets. She licks her lips, and before I know it I'm on my bike and speeding away into broken pavements veneered by the summer sun.

'Kalki!' I shout, throwing my bike onto the ground and running up the veranda steps. He's shirtless, moody and his ringletted hair is all over the place.

'What?'

'That girl… she's…' I'm panting, but there's no time to catch my breath. 'Just go to the temple…. my family temple… she's there and she's… there's blood everywhere!'

I know I don't make sense, but he's had experience with horrified people so he can understand what I'm trying to say. 'Can I borrow your bike?' he asks. I nod. 'Stay here, okay? Until I get back.' He disappears into the forest.

I wait outside the house, because going in alone would mean a lot of things that I don't want to deal with right now. What I saw is still weighing on my mind. I want to ignore the well on the side, but the more I try not to look at it the more I do.

Before I know it I'm looking right into the water, my palms spreading over the slabs. They look like tombstones. That's when I realize how much I hate this well. I will do anything to seal it. It took away my best friend, it ruined us. I want to bend down and call her name. Just to know how loud my echo is. Just to know if she will call my name back.

If I just jump, will she break my fall?

Go back right now, Noor. My mind screams at me. I know how perilous this is and it is either terrible grief or something else that is making my mind foggy. I take a few steps back, then some more, and now I'm far enough to know that I've been lured.

Angry with myself for not having control, I stalk back to the front door and sit on the steps. There is a big photo of Krishna uncle on the wall and I stare at it. What kind of relationship did these two siblings have with their father? Was it tumultuous? I knew Kirti hated her father, but now I know Kalki did too. But then, why did he follow the same profession?

Why must it run in the family? Doesn't anyone in this little village even dare to be different?

It is sunset by the time Kalki gets back. He's brought me food and he's apologizing profusely for making me stay so late. 'I didn't think it would take this long.'

'Why do you look shaken?'

'I don't know. I just saw a half-eaten child.'

'Wait, what?'

For the first time he looks agitated. He curses himself for what he's just said to me and shakes his head. 'I'm sorry, that was uncalled for. I shouldn't have been so blunt. I'm just...'

I wait for him to pick his words up, trying to hide my horror. But I'm mortified just looking at him quiver.

'I don't know how to forget what I just saw.'

'What do you mean?'

'Whatever you saw...' he begins and my spine turns ice. I know what I saw and I've been swallowing back bile ever since.

'… was her eating an actual person?' I ask. 'What?!'

I am a slab of jelly. There is nothing in me that feels like it can handle this. I want to throw up, but my mouth isn't even working. My jaw is transfixed.

He nods, a little pale. 'They're cremating the child right now. I don't know how the pendants came off, I'd told her never to remove it.'

He smells like guilt. Reeking of self-reproach. It looks like he's taking responsibility for what's happened even though none of it is his fault. I know someone's said something during this series of events and I ask him.

'They're just saying the usual stuff. They need to blame someone,' he says.

'So someone did say something?' I ask.

He grunts. And tries to walk past me, but I block his way. We are not done with this.

'What did they say?' I ask.

'Well. One of the villagers. A usual troublemaker. He was just opening guilt traps. Saying that if I had been more careful I would have saved the child. That I was careless, that the girl was careless, he repeats.'

I am angry at whoever is spreading this nasty comment and I swear loudly. But anger has no role here. I can tell he is upset.

'There's more to this, isn't there?'

He nods, rueful and self-conscious. 'Yes,' he says. 'The village chief and the board spoke to me today. They're trying to get me to stop practicing black magic, because...'

'Because they're blaming you?'

He nods again. 'Yes. They think I'm just like my father.'

'Well, you're not,' I say, indignant.

'They don't understand that I'm not inviting the ghosts, I'm driving them away. If it weren't for me there'd be more evil here.' He sighs. 'And it's not my fault my ancestors brought so many evil forces into this world, into this village. I'm sorry, I'm really sorry about it. But god, I've tried so much to undo all that and repay their sins. This weight that I carry with me, it doesn't even belong to me.'

'But the villagers, they know you're helping them. They treat you with more respect than all those people who head the village,' I say, defending him.

He smiles a bit. 'Well. That's their problem. They don't like to see someone who isn't part of their team with so much power. They know how much trust the villagers put in me. They can't even gather half that trust for themselves.'

I burst out laughing. 'So they're just jealous.'

He's washing his hands with the pipe outside the veranda now. It feels like he's lightened up a bit and I am glad. I hate this bullying, this ostracism and ridicule. The best people keep having to put up with it. He washes his face and the kohl leaks down his face. Once he is done wiping his face he looks up at me and says something I will never forget.

'Isn't it a damn shame? All of us want to change the world.' He's looking up, the sunlight dripping down his chin like honey. 'All of us want to make it a better place, make it our place. Eventually it's all about ruling, overthrowing, empowering and endangering. All these people, whether they're village chiefs, Panchayat heads or politicians, they just want to turn it all around. Nobody is trying to save us. And nobody is trying to save the world. The only thing the world needs saving from is us. People. And we're such dumb puppets, we think all these people with words of silk and buttered up speeches can help us get to a better place. It's all power play here, Noor. People want to rule the villagers. Ghosts want to rule the villagers. Gods want to rule. There is so much competition and there is so much greed. All of them are fighting for this land, for control over it and for control over people. Some of them show love and extend a helping hand. Like the friendly ghosts. And some of them attack and force their power onto the proletariat, like the evil spirits. Like the *vetala* you saw. It probably couldn't have done much harm, but it certainly wanted to scare you away. They're all hungry for control. For possession. Tell me just how different are we from them? How badly have we ever wanted mutual harmony? We've only wanted to possess too, to possess other people, to own them, to make them ours and to rule them. I'm always getting confused with who the real monsters are.'

'Are you scared?' I ask him.

'What do you mean?'

'Do you think the village holds you accountable for things that go wrong? I mean, what happens if you make a mistake?'

His mouth is a bitter line. 'Well, I'm not god,' he spits. 'But I'm not a monster either. I'm human. So god help me, I get to make mistakes. I get to make mistakes and not be judged for it. I deserve at least that much and I deserve to be forgiven. I don't want to be held accountable for being a human being. I will admit it is my fault, but I will also move on from it. Why doesn't anybody understand this, goddammit?

Why are we celebrating ourselves so much and fixing ideals when we should just be living our lives and doing whatever we want? What is the point of all this pressure? My god, life is so simple. So very simple. We make it difficult, don't we? We make it into something that kills us and drives us crazy. All I want is to lie on my easy chair, smoke some hookah or have some good coffee, home made with a little extra caffeine, and read a good book, possibly Plato or Rousseau.'

I put my arm around him. He is taken aback, but covers it up. We stay that way for a long time and I know he has begun to feel better.

'Don't let them do that to you,' I say. 'There are places in you that don't believe in anything anymore. I'm scared of that. When I see you look so empty, so lifeless, I am terrified. What have they done to you? Why are they onto you? You never did anything wrong. I don't want you to feel this way. Don't let them bring you down.' I've never seen him vulnerable and it melts me. Men think it's so important to be stoic and stone cold, but honestly, it's when they're unarmed and sensitive that they're most beautiful. I like this side to him, it makes me less intimidated by all that he is. I keep my arm around him for a while, comfortable with the light intimacy.

'They?' he asks, smiling.

'They. Whoever they are.'

'Are we still talking about the villagers?'

'I don't know.'

He just chuckles. We haven't talked like this before, so fluid, so easy, uninhibited, like this is where we were always meant to be — sitting by each other, talking about us and the world.

'What was she doing in my temple anyway?' I ask, inquisitive.

'That place has been isolated for years now. It's a good hiding spot.'

'But it's a temple!' I exclaim. 'It's asylum for humans. The monsters can't touch us there! God lives there.'

He chuckles. 'Is that so?'

'You don't believe in god?'

He shrugs. 'I don't know what my beliefs are. Nietzche once said, God is dead. But I'd like to believe some bastard's out there protecting me. That would be downright nice.'

I chuckle. 'Crude, but okay.'

He laughs with me. 'Anyway, like I said, the temple is empty. Nobody has prayed there for a while so it's lost its power.'

'But…' I'm still not convinced.

He puts both hands on my shoulder and says, 'Noor. Your fixed ideologies are going to bog you down. What if it's not black and white? What if everything is a blur? Do you read about your gods or the texts written for them? Look at the Mahabharat. Yudhishtir is Yama's son, son of a god, so righteous and good, and he still barters his wife like she is an object, a possession. Look at Greek mythology. Zeus rapes Leda as a swan. You have horny gods, bad gods, gods who make mistakes. You have humans, good men, bad men. And then, you have the others. They're supposed to be bad, these spirits, these demons. But what do we know? We know nothing. We always try to write our own stories so there's some history, something set in stone, so it's not the unknown. Because what we fear most is the unknown.' He takes a deep breath and looks me in the eye. 'What I'm trying to say is, anything is possible. Gods. Monsters. Anyone can be a god. And anyone can be a monster.'

Chapter Ten

When the torrent speaks to us it speaks in a rage. It is pouring and I am in the temple again. But this time I'm with him. The rain is washing away the blood and I don't know how, but my hand is in his.

'My grandmother used to come here every morning,' I whisper.

He nods. 'It's a lovely place. Derelict, but lovely nonetheless.'

'I still can't believe I saw someone eat a human. That is real, live cannibalism.'

'Just try not to think about it.'

'It was in a temple. Is nowhere safe?'

'London is safe for you. You should go back to Maggie's place.'

I stiffen. I whip my head around at him and he knows he's caught.

'What?' I grab both his hands and imprison him. 'What did you just say?'

I'm angry now. There is so much he knows and I feel exposed. I'm not scared, because by now I know that I'm safe with him. I talk to the villagers and they tell me he is their protector, their little god. But I don't want him to know so much about me when I haven't figured a thing about him.

I hate that he is a mystery and I an open book.

It worries me how quickly I've started falling for him. Love is this glorious candlelight dinner a sick teenager pukes out so that she can stay skinny. I know the consequences and I know it is addictive. I don't want to get tangled up.

But I like him. I like how there's a quiet place inside of him that's vulnerable and soft and real. I like how my heart knocks into my chest every time I'm around him. I like his ghost stories and his antidotes and his half smile.

'How do you know about Maggie?' I ask.

I want us to be secret diaries to each other. It can't be a one way street. I need to know things — about him, about his family, about everything. How long will I be kept in the dark? I like him so much, so damn much, if only I can tell. But I won't, because even thinking of liking him scares me.

'Tell me why you know so much!' I scream at him. Now I'm angry. It's the damn rain, it won't stop, and I feel like we're standing in a graveyard. The place looks that haunted and deserted. It's always been, I realize.

Was there anything to come back to anyway?

'I just do!'

'Did you do some hocus pokus to find out? Some weird crystal gazing?'

'What? No!' He's angry now too, I can tell from the way his eyes flash. His hair is matted on his forehead and he has never looked this bewitching to me. But he can't just keep doing this to me. I know nothing about him and he knows everything about me and I hate it. 'I know so much because… because.'

'Because *what*?'

'Because I've always liked you, okay?'

'What?'

He is breathing heavily, his eyebrows stitched together, seeping into each other like marshy lake outlets. He unties his hair and it spills over his face, full of riddles, like a crest of lavish carbon.

'Stop looking so innocent, Noor. You can't tell me you don't know how beautiful you are. You've always been, even as a little girl, when you were hanging around my sister and the rare occasions you came home. I always saw you when I was back home for the holidays and you made me crazy. So crazy that I wasn't even allowed to touch you. Nobody would even let me go near you, you were so protected. My parents would have killed me if I even spoke to you.'

'What?'

He's moving closer now and my feet have rooted themselves to the ground.

'You could have spoken to me,' I say sheepishly. I don't know why, but my heart is jumping out. 'You know I didn't believe in all that. Caste, class, whatever.'

'Are you kidding me?' He laughs. 'Our entire history is a chronology of class and caste struggles. You were Noor, such a princess, kept hidden from the rest of the world. I was surprised they even let you play with Kirti, probably because you made a big fuss about it. I loved that about you. How you got so fierce when you crusaded for your best friend.' He looks up at me.

'You were so loyal to her. And I was the spawn of Satan, just a poor boy trying to reach for the stars and getting nothing but the dark arts. Nothing but curses and prejudice and everyone's hate. *Of course* I couldn't touch you, Noor. It was as if you built the sky. What does that even mean to someone who came from hell?'

You can touch me now, my body pleads. I push the thought back.

'So yes, when you left Herga I asked her,' he goes on. 'I asked her all the time about you. When you texted her that night I texted you back. I missed you. Shit, I know it's a horrible thing to do, text from a dead girl's phone, that too my sister's, but fuck okay, I've never stopped.'

'Never stopped what?' I ask, my breath caught midway in my throat.

'Loving you.'

I close the gap between us and pull his head towards me.

We are kissing in the rain and I'm dying. His hands try to close around my waist like broken clasps. I know he's been craving me since the day he saw me arrive in Herga, but I didn't think it went as far to our childhoods. His hands on me build a tribal bonfire into my skin. There's always something left to lose.

Always. This time it's arrived in eyes that look like fatal mountaineering accidents and breaths that fall on my skin like rose petal confetti. I'm wearing my heart on my sleeve, for all the villagers to see, and I don't give a damn. I have no doubt that he's a magician. I'm already spellbound. I'm not going to even fight him. I might just love him. For a fleeting moment I think of Amma and Baba. Guilt ransacks me. But I can't resist him and I know I've let them down. But none of it matters. He's here, he's holding me. Nobody's ever called me beautiful to my face and nobody's ever looked at me like I was water to parched throats, spring to flowers on the asphalt. I have no clue what will happen to me, I'm caught in such an alluring trap.

But I'm his by default. It's not like I have a choice.

I don't know if love is enough to save us, if love is enough for anything at all. I'm scared, so scared. But I come so badly undone inside his brick roof arms. I'm safe and I don't care for the world.

I'm not too stupid, I tell myself. I know this isn't going to last, forever is a pretty lie we've patterned ourselves into. I already see myself on a train in England, a Marquez book in my hand as I look out the window for things that pass me by discreetly, and I wonder if I'll ever be the same.

There's nothing called forever. Forevers come with

expiry dates.

He's going to stay back and I'm going to leave and we'll mess it up. He looks at me like a wounded animal, because I've suddenly stopped kissing him. My head is spinning, cartwheeling even. God, I'm such a fool.

I pull back and push him away. He's still disoriented and confused, but I don't say anything. I turn around and run away into the woods. He calls my name, but I don't look back.

All my life I've been running from things. Acceptance mostly.

My best friend is dead and I kissed my dead best friend's brother. Shouldn't I be mad at him for faking her identity and texting me from her phone? I'm mad at myself for not being mad at him.

The idea of having feelings for someone I just shouldn't is scarring me to my bones, yet again. Something tells me that I always make the worst of decisions.

Noor, you fool. I whisper softly. *You never learn. You never learn to shield yourself from anything that is wrong, anyone who may be wrong. You always manage to fall for the wrong boy.*

As I run all I can think about is his kiss and all those conversations in his room about Nietzsche and Sartre and Derrida. It's so confusing. He's brilliant and well-read, yet he's dabbling in all this nonsense. I don't understand if what the villagers say are just rumours. But they tell me he's the one they go to for exorcisms. He lures the spirits out of humans and traps them in pendants and trees and other things. He has his own methods. They tell me he's not human, that he's sold his soul to the devil. And then, some tell me that he's a good man and a good black magician. That he helps people come out of possession and that he does only good deeds. That he's not like his father, using magic for evil. But there is a curse on that family. They've been trading with spirits for generations. Bad things happen to them and everyone associated with them. That's something everyone in the village is sure of.

As I stand in the heart of my hometown I realize how big a part of me it is. How I'm just like everyone else even though I left a long while back. I'm naïve and simple and complicated like them.

We were the people who saw the dead. A ghost town.

We lost our gods. Our smiles. Our morals. Our breaths. Our friends. Our words. Our voices. Our hearts. Our homes. Our fathers. Our land. Our favourite songs. Our handwritten letters. Our minds. Ourselves. But when I kissed him today I knew there was so much more to lose.

I still have something left to lose.

I'm so caught up with my thoughts that I don't see a branch fall before me. My feet stop moving forward. I have done something awful to myself. I have led myself into a dangerous place and I am alone.

I don't know where I am.

Something somewhere starts singing and I have a feeling it is right behind me.

Every hair on me is rising. In the heat of Herga the coldest thing is my body. It feels like someone is snatching my breath away. I start running again.

Kirti once told me never to look back if I ever felt I was being followed. Whatever was following me couldn't get to me unless I turned around and saw it. I don't know how true this is, but I need it most at the moment. I'm running so fast my legs feel like gelatin. My feet are growing sore and there is no breath left in me. Another branch falls in front of me and there is a loud cackle.

I'm so terrified.

I close my eyes and start to pray. But I don't know

if Muslim prayers count in a Hindu village. But God will hear me. Someone will hear me. I am shivering. I've never felt this cold, not even in London during winter, when everything turned to ice.

I'm dying and I'm praying for the first time in my life.

I have to wake up and save myself. I want to open my eyes, but I'm scared something might be standing in front of me. This time it won't be a branch I'm sure.

Kirti, please help me.

The singing is in sync with laughter. An orchestra of humming and hysterics. Wild, uncontrollable laughter. I can't tell if it's a child or a woman, but I don't know which is worse.

And then, suddenly, there are paws running over dead leaves. I know what animals they are from, their growls.

Wolves.

I open my eyes and I see them. Surrounding me and growling at something. They've encircled me, like a Lakshman rekha, and they're all facing away from me. I don't move. I'm not safe, I'm still not. I won't feel safe until I see him.

And then, he emerges from between two trees,

he's looking right into what the wolves are looking at. I don't understand. What do they see that I don't?

And the air, it is suddenly so still. I can't feel anything move, not even the trees, which were swaying so much in the wind, their barks dead and dancing. 'Kalki,' I choke out and the wolves make way for him to get to me.

I begin to cry and suddenly his expression softens. 'Come with me, it'll be okay.'

'Will you stay with me tonight in Ajja's house?'

'I'm not allowed into your Ajja's house,' he says. 'They forbade me. We are all forbidden. By birth. I can't, Noor.' I never realized what his family was to the society. They were all isolated because of their father.

I want to tell him that they're dead, that it's okay for him to come in. But I know he's promised them and to someone like him only their bodies are dead. He will never break the pact. So instead I tell him, 'Can I come to your place then?'

He looks surprised. 'Won't that affect you? I mean…'

'Kirti and her mother died in that well. Yes, I'm petrified. But I know I've got you.'

The longest distance between us is just a

wavelength. I try to pick myself up, still stumbling over the two things that happened today. One, a dream. The other, a night terror. I'm constantly bridging the gap between the two like a portal. I'll never sleep peacefully again, not if I hear that insidious laugh again. I need him by my side, I know I don't even know him well, but it just feels so right, so safe.

'I can't keep saving you,' he drawls, twirling one of my wayward locks between his fingers. 'What you did just now was unforgivable. It put you at risk and I don't ever want that.' He suddenly looks sad. 'You'll be safer without me around.'

'What do you mean?'

'They were after you because of me.'

'They?'

He doesn't say anything. I'm so annoyed now. I can't believe that we've come this far and he still doesn't talk to me about the trade. I don't even know if I'll believe half of it, but still. It's just not fair.

'Why won't you tell me?'

'Because I can't.'

'That's not a good enough reason.'

'I can't offer you another one. It's all I have.'

'Kalki…'

'I can't.'

My palms are on his cheeks and I'm watching him clenching and unclenching as he tries to calm himself down. I'm a mess too, I'm a mess on the verge of collapsing. He says he's been in love with me ever since we were children, but he doesn't open up to me at all. What's he scared of?

'I want to know.'

'No.'

'Please, I'm begging you.'

'It's all started with that miserable, lowlife well!' he yells. I have never seen him this agonized. 'I can't explain this feeling, Noor. There are times when that disgusting well just gets to me. I want to seal it for mental satisfaction. It doesn't make sense. If closing it means never being able to retrieve that sack then I shouldn't even think of closing it. But deep down it disturbs me. I want to keep telling myself that the well didn't do anything to kill my sister and my mother, but I still hate it. I want to destroy it. Just as much as you do. I want to teach it a lesson and I want to finish it off and I... hell, I just want to run away from here. I hate this place. It took everything away from me. And it'll take you too if I'm not careful. This whole place is haunted, cursed, call it whatever you want. And so am I.'

I want to ask him so many things. What sack? He wants to leave? Leave this place for good? What does he mean he's cursed? Nothing rings a bell, only makes me feel feeble.

By now he looks so sad and tortured that I can't help but put my arms around him again. 'I don't want to lose you.' I know where this is headed. Everyone I've tried to save has only ever hurt me in the end.

But there's really no going back now, is there?

'Don't fall for me, Noor. I'm not what you think I am. I feel so guilty already, god, you have no idea how I feel. This thing between us should never have unravelled.'

'I don't think anything,' I say, kissing his shoulder. 'I only think about wanting you. I only want you.'

'I've only ever wanted you,' he sighs. 'But as long as you're with me you'll never be safe.'

'Tell me now, who was that woman in the red sari?'

I wait for him to answer me, but he doesn't reply. 'Kalki?'

'Rakteswari.'

He's given me a name. I can't ask him for more. He's not supposed to give out family trade secrets like that and I understand. I decide to keep silent and instead ask Gopi's wife about this other woman. She would definitely know.

Chapter Eleven

The sky is a spread of rose quartz and ballet shoes. Geraniums and cherry coke. Bubble gum sticks to the mackerel clouds that spread over it. It is going to be dark and I need to be back home like I promised.

Do you think this well is bigger than the one in your house? She asks me. I'm tying my hair with candycane ribbons and smiling at her. Of course, it is! I cry and we both giggle. This is what we do. Smile, laugh and hold hands. Run, sing and dance. We are children and we know nothing.

Her house has the biggest well in the village, but nobody ever takes water from it. I don't know why, it is such a beautiful well. There are runes embedded on the rocks and we've spent so much of our time tracing them and trying to interpret them. And then, either her father or that brother of hers would come running out of the house telling us to stay away from it.

Why? Kirti would ask, her lower lip jutting out.

Just like that, you silly twat, the young boy with messy bedroom hair would say, pushing her shoulder a little, his eyes fixated on me.

And then, I'd run off, remembering what my parents had told me. Run if you see him. Run as far as you can. He is no good, don't even let him stare at you.

Even the ghosts are safer. The last thing you want, Noor, is to be possessed by a human.

And now here I am, possessed by the very same. And I am not afraid anymore. I can't be.

Suddenly, I want everything that this has to offer us.

I want to be alive at the time of night when he's beside me, sleeping, breathing softly as his stressful nights melt into lucid dreams. I want to be alive for the nights when he will wake up crying about things that don't make sense to him, when I tell him it will be alright. I don't comprehend how I am so closely welded with someone from a world I know so little about. I don't think about what could happen to us if we dive further. We'd probably end up tangled and cut up for everyone to see. I can already feel myself being knitted into a microscope. The village is watching us through its 7 pm power cuts and old temples. It wonders, what an odd friendship. Somehwere in the neighbourhood, prayers are being offered. A ghost leans against the bark of a tree and hums an old Tulu song, a little off-pitch. The butterflies in my stomach are making their way up my throat. I look up at him, and goosebumps fall on me like early morning dew. I like him more than I've liked anything at all. And I just can't explain it. I just want to feel like this forever, and if this moment is all I will get, then so be it. Beautiful things don't stay anyway. Nothing does, actually.

'Are you sure about this, Noor?' he asks me. 'Are you sure about me?'

'What do you mean?'

He looks shy, a little awkward. 'I don't think I'm what you're looking for. That's all. You deserve better.'

Somewhere in the distant horizon the thunder throws a tantrum at the sky. I can hear birds flying back to their homes. I'm so at peace with the silence and the sight of his serene face searching my eyes for answers. Imploring, begging. *Please say you want me.*

'I never looked for anything, Kalki,' I begin slowly. 'I crashed into it, I clawed my way into it, I crawled towards it. If I want you, I want you. I have never looked for anything until I actually found it. And I am glad I found you.'

I stand on tip toe and kiss his cheek. He's still very confused, like he's been thinking the whole night about what to say and he hasn't got it out completely. I don't let him say anything. I don't want anything to ruin this for me. For us.

And so there it begins. I don't know what I've signed up for. All I know is that I want him, and he wants me.

'Do you like me or do you… love me?' I ask hesitantly.

He smiles. 'Guess it's love.'

I burst out laughing. The word floats above us, hovers. The day is slowly stripteasing its way into dusk. Soft moonlight makes teeth marks on his bare back.

'Why?'

'Why I love you?'

I nod.

He takes a deep breath. 'I think I have always loved you, because you looked like you wouldn't hurt me. You looked so happy all the time, like you'd even love an ugly little moth if it sat on your shoulder. I felt like such a sharp contrast. Dark. Cold. A swamp of trash born in the wrong family. Like an untouchable. Hell, I was an untouchable, still am. You loved everything, everyone, you were without boundaries. And I, I was a border. Still am. Never in my craziest fantasies have I dreamt that one day you'd be in my arms, looking at me like that, like I mean something to you. What I'd give to relive this very moment a thousand times. In threescore years and ten, and forever after, my heart will never stop beating for you.'

*

I wear his hands to sleep that night. Fireflies build rings around his fingers as they slide over me.

I get tongue tied on calls to my mother ever since. What would I say anyway? Mother, once I saw a man weep into his hands and there, between his cold palms, he discovered magic. Mother, he healed people and yet they were afraid of him.

Mother, I am afraid of him.

I imagine her walking away from me. Daadi, Baba, everyone. You can have him, but you can't have us, they'll say. I try to explain and fail.

'What're you thinking?' he whispers, grinning.

'About you,' I say, still wondering if he can read my thoughts.

'Good. I like your face when you're thinking of me.'

'And otherwise?' I ask cheekily.

'Otherwise too. Always.'

It goes on like this. He says the nicest of things. But then, there are moments when he realizes what is going on, when the reality of it finally settles in, and he is intimidated. He doesn't know where this will go, but he knows it will break him if it doesn't go far. If it doesn't make it to the end. And that is when the problem begins. When he sees that and tries to repel and dispute.

Every time I ask about the woman he is defensive. It has been a week now and he's finally found the courage to show me Kirti's letters to her mother.

Amma, I saw you in my dreams again last night.

Amma, you rose up from the well and you were screaming.

I wear your sari sometimes. I miss you.

He doesn't read them. I think it's something

he can't admit, that he's devastated by her death. I remember the night I found out she was gone. I dealt with loss in the most heartbreaking way. I denied it.

He tells me about their childhood. How they grew up in a family that the village feared and despised. He talks about Kirti crying because kids at school bullied her for being the black magician's daughter. Nostalgia is a dripping tap in an old house. My memories lay splattered on its steps. I quietly clean up, leaving behind a lamplit melancholy that looks back at me accusingly. Noor, the girl in your past is gone, it says.

'She's not coming back,' I finally admit and he nods, staring into the distance.

'I felt less lonely when you texted her. I thought I was the only one grieving for so long, but then, you sent that message and… my god, Noor, I couldn't believe it.'

'I loved her.'

'Me too, in my own ridiculous way.' He sighs. 'You don't realize how broken you are until you're broken. That fleeting moment when a completely normal glass becomes shards — it's so small. Before you know it, you're on your knees, on the ground, in pieces. And you think, oh shit, now what? My father's been killed by ghosts, my mother and sister killed themselves and

I'm caught up in a curse that never lets me go.'

I wonder what he means by the last bit, but I don't ask. I grip his hand tightly instead.

'Don't dwell on it.'

He laughs. 'You're right. Life is, ultimately, an existential play Camus wrote. It makes no sense and yet it is there.'

Meanwhile, in this hot and cold, the weather continues to play mind games with us. At times I am at the highest peak of London's shard, looking down at lights and skyscrapers, and at times I am buried underground, sinking to a low even the Bermuda triangle cannot suck me into. He does that to me. I should have known not to play with fire, with magic. I seem to have lost sight of why I came here, but it feels like I was meant to come here only to find him.

Sometimes he pulls me close and makes me feel loved. And sometimes he is distant, detached, almost as if he is fighting it.

'I know it's difficult for you to tell me a lot of these things, because they're all family secrets,' I confess, my eyes pooling. 'But can you blame me for wanting to know? I've got so close to you and yet you're so far. How do I make ends meet?'

'You can't, Noor. This is a mistake. I should never have told you that I liked you. You shouldn't have kissed me.'

'Then why did you send your wolves after me? You could have left me to die.'

'They were after you because of me!' he claims angrily.

'Who? Just tell me what we're running away from!' I yell back at him. We've been having the same conversation for over a week now and he refuses to tell me anything about his life or the woman in the red sari.

'Noor, I don't want you to get hurt.'

'I'm not…' Before I know it I'm flying right into him. 'Just tell me! Why won't you tell me?' I say, clutching the front of his shirt and looking up at him with accusing eyes.

We're on edge now and I can feel his heart beat, light years away from me, echoing back the same screams, the same fears that I have.

'Why are you pushing me away now?' I sob.

Gopi's wife warned me. Her warnings reverberate in my head. The first time I'd just been intimidated. The second, right after she'd found out I was spending way too much time with him and she'd admonished me again, I'd just been fascinated.

But now I worry. I worry he's going to leave.

There's a long silence. His jaw is clenching and unclenching. Here I am, I think, picking fights with a man whose mask knows him better than I do when there's war back home. My people are now collateral damage. Helplessness and guilt stack up in front of me like unfinished paperwork. I've no weapons to fight with. Just a thread of hope through a series of phone calls to my family.

When my mother asks me if I'm okay, I lie. Take me back I want to say, now that he's acting irrational. Go back to when you had me and build me an iron wall. I'm too weak for this world. Mother, I'm not ready for his love.

'You don't want me around,' I say angrily.

'Yes! I don't want you around, Noor!' he yells. 'Just go home! It's not right for me to even touch you!'

We're flung into another long silence. He expects me to walk away, crying, but I know what he wants from this. He's lying to me so that he can scare me away and protect me. I can see through his plan and I'm not going to fall for it.

I look him square in the eye. 'I want you to touch me. Over and over again.'

'Shit, don't say things like that.' But I know I've already enchanted him. His eyes are aflame. Twin torches. 'Please. Go home.'

'I was, until you showed up. Now it's all a mess.'

'We're a mess. We're not right. I mean it, I don't want you,' he says and looks away.

'You want me and then you don't want me. What's all this about?' I ask him. 'You're lying, Kalki. Just spit it out, tell me what they're doing to you.'

'I can't. But, Noor, I'll always want you.' He takes a deep breath, trying to refine his words. 'But… but you're going to get hurt if you're with me. They're going to do something to you and I won't be able to save you.'

He keeps talking about them, but I don't know who they are and he won't tell me.

'You can't stay away from me. Do you think this is a coincidence, me coming back to Herga after so many years? You've waited for this all along and now you're saying you don't want this?'

He walks over to the hookah and begins to prepare the coal. I watch the bubbles in the vessel rise as he puts the pipe to his mouth. For a long time he doesn't even answer me. He is lost in his thoughts again and lost to me. And then, he speaks.

'You used to play in the fields a lot. And when you saw me there, your eyes, already so huge, would widen even more. You looked so funny and yet so adorable. There was nothing on your face except eyes, I swear. Big, round eyes, so terrified of me. Then you'd run off, tripping over your long skirt, tripping over the stones, but you'd never look back at me. Not even once.'

'But what did I do?' I ask him desperately. 'What did I do for you to even like me? I never even spoke to you.'

He shrugs. 'You just looked... so innocent, Noor. So pathetically innocent that anyone would want to pick you up and scoop you into their arms. And for someone like me, who couldn't even dream of you, you were my weakness, the chink in my armour, my vulnerability.' He touches my cheek. 'And, Noor, you have a face that would make even the most heartless of demons want to protect you.'

'So that's it?' I chuckle. 'You just want what you can't have?'

He shakes his head. 'I like your hands.'

I raise my eyebrows. 'My hands?'

He traces the line right below the lifeline. 'You're an artist now, aren't you? That's so beautiful. What do you paint?'

'Things nobody can see.'

'Like?'

'Loneliness.'

'Are you going to be lonely if I'm gone?'

He showed up suddenly and everything was wonderful in my life. When he talks about leaving I die a little. I think about how I felt when Kirti left me. Empty. Misery too, at some point, is guilty pleasure to someone who's gone absolutely numb. And what I'd give to feel anything at all. So I threw myself into self destruction.

If he leaves I don't think I can handle it.

'You love me right?'

He nods.

'Then why?' I ask him. I don't know why he is blocking me out. Is it going to be like this then, a stretch of ups and downs? Will I be eating fire and swallowing ice? 'What if… what if I tell you that I love you too? Just as much as you love me? How much ever it is.'

For a few seconds he is stumped. And then, he says sadly, almost as if it's too late, 'Love can't save all of us. And there are too many of us.'

Chapter Twelve

'You deserve to live a life free of fear.' he says.

'And of love?' I ask him bitterly.

I can't sacrifice, and I can't give him up. There's nothing to do but to keep walking, even if we are leading each other to dead ends.

'I will never belong in your world just as much as you wouldn't in mine. I don't know what else to say, I'm sorry. I know it looks like I've led you on, but trust me, okay? I really want you. I love you so much I can't put you in danger. I'm going down, but I just can't drag you along. Nothing can redeem me now. Not even your light. Have you seen a firefly, Noor? The tiniest bodies can have the fiercest of lights. But they're still tiny, they're still vulnerable. A firefly can only dream of illuminating the entire village with its brightness. But the night is long and dark and it can only go on for so long. And this darkness, Noor, will crush the living daylight out of you. I am warning you now, please, just leave.'

'No,' I refuse, holding him tight. He doesn't push me away, but he doesn't hug me back either. 'No,' I repeat. 'No, no, no.'

'Noor.'

'Don't ask me to leave, Kalki. Just don't. You leave if you want to. But don't you dare ask me to leave. I can't do it. It's not in me to do it.'

He cups my cheek. 'You don't get it at all, do you?'

'Is it so wrong to hope?'

'I don't know, Noor. I don't know anything anymore.'

'We can only try,' I whisper and grab his hand. Pulling him into the room, I watch him follow me, entranced. He wants to know if I am sure about this. But I am. I have never felt this sure all my life.

'Noor,' he says, his voice husky.

'Shh. This is for us.'

I blush to deep carmine when he watches me undress with comet taupe eyes, fierce and spitting flames. He looks like he could devour me, but I'm not afraid this time. I have never done this before and I have never felt so bold. It's like he's got full control over my body and there's nothing I can do but turn helpless lumber puppet in his arms. His breath catches in his throat when he realizes what I'm doing and he takes a few steps closer. He looks like this is all he's ever wanted, all his life. Just me. His eyes can't get enough, ever since they laid themselves on the little girl with rosette and swan lake ribbons, to the now, fresh lavender skin basking in full womanly glory. He's believed in the worst of ghosts, but he can't believe this. He doesn't blink. He closes the curtains, because he doesn't want a ray of light to see me, he is that possessive. My pashmina shawl and leggings have formed a pool around my bare legs. I'm pulling up my top. When it reaches my head my elbows are caught in them and I can feel strong arms encircle my waist. With my top I am in his arms. I have looked for art in so many of Europe's finest galleries but never seen anything so quiet and yet insanely expressive as his face. His hair is pulled back into a small pony. I want to undress it, rip the hair band apart and run my fingers through them. Ripples of unruly *manna*. Pulling and tugging and dissolving into myself. I don't understand where this courage is coming from, but there are tiny explosions in my head.

'Kiss me,' I hiss when his lips touch my neck. 'Just... yes.' His hands are experts, peppered with skill, and they draw on me gently at first, then roughly. He suddenly picks me up and carries me into his room.

He lays me on the mattress, a patchwork of delicate hyacinths, and I lie there watching him, intoxicated and befuddled. 'Kalki…'

'You're so sweet and nice and… *god.*' He unbuttons his jeans. 'Even a second with you, Noor, is a lifetime of bliss.'

My heart sinks. Through this fever a scary thought latches onto me.

This is temporary. Very, very temporary.

His eyes look back into mine wistfully. He knows exactly what I'm thinking. And he doesn't say a word.

He doesn't say a word and I'm shattered.

*

The night is a star goddess. She looks down at the lone house that is a refuge to the two lovers curled beside each other. His hands are on my waist and mine are on his chest. I'm counting his eyelashes. He's watching me play with him. And now I know how everything has led back to this. From watching untouchable things at a distance, it was all about finding him, hating him, throwing water balloons at him, writing poetry for each other, touching him, watching him touch me, loving him, telling him what a comfort he was, screaming his name in the dark, wanting him, blowkissing his soft river cheeks, secretly wishing he'd call, running back to him after the worst of times and dissolving into his butterfinger fudge arms. It was always, always about starting with him, meandering into his steep valleys and fighting gargoyles, stealing sweets from the earthenware candy jar, growing fresh bells of Ireland and Amaryllis together. And it was always about ending with him. Never a neat circle, a hedge maze, and he was the illusion of a door that I never got to open. But he loved me even as a child. And I loved his messy hair, the hitch in his breath, his water-lorn hiccups, the way he tips his head back when he laughs and his angry gash of a mouth, full and deliciously mine. I loved his early morning eyes, his late night voice and everything in between. It was my fate, written in the stars maybe, that every road ever walked by my helpless feet would lead to him. From Herga to Kashmir, to London, to Herga again. It's like telepathy, like he sings to me from oceans away and the clouds carry his tune back to me and I know, I just know the lyrics by heart. This is the only pilgrimage I need for my homeless soul, a long journey in discovery of an untapped world of colours in him, him, him and only him, my crusade, my holy expedition. From him to all the nonsense we put each other through, chasing after slamming doors, beating shut eyes under 4 am skies, playing rummy in his room and placing drunk calls to him. It all leads back only to him.

That night I watch him sleep. I can't get the image out of my head. This is how we spend most of our time. Under the sheets, toe over toe, talking. Getting to know each other. Taking turns cooking and learning more than each other's names. Filling up the gaps that years have left, for all the years that kept us apart. There is no small talk between us. Only extremes. It is either silence or flaming discussions about politics, society, economy, art and everything under the sky. Sometimes we are in the fields chasing each other and pushing ourselves into the river. Sometimes we are in houses, invited to *kolas* and sometimes outdoors, watching *kambalas*, the bull races. Sometimes we are just taking quiet walks and enjoying the scenic appeal of Herga. And sometimes we are in our room, eye to eye, engrossed in debates about mythology and reality.

'What bothers you most about reality?' I ask him.

'That we need dreams to exist in it. He says. If we don't have an imagination, a world we can escape into, then we're all going to go mad. All of us. This whole world as one big mental asylum. Can you imagine that?'

'I think so,' I say. He touches my head with his grapevine fingers, plays with a coil of my hair. I try explaining to him what art means to me. As an artist, my heart is half paint, a layover for sketches and empty canvases.

For a long while both of us are restful within private quarters of our own minds. I am humming and he is back to his hookah, and the room fills with a pleasant fruit smell.

'Haven't you ever thought about leaving this place?' I ask him, remembering what he said earlier.

A long pause. 'No.'

'Why not?'

'Even thinking about it is dangerous. Hoping. Hoping even a little bit could ruin me.'

I don't say anything to that. A sense of profound despair sticks to my bones. Maybe this is one question I should never ask again.

I have never seen a man look so broken until now.

Chapter Thirteen

Cold ash on his forehead like a summer deity. A chalk of cigarette dust on his shirt. His snake an idol worshipping his neck like its own temple. I've never met a philosopher as brilliant as him. He took me to his library once. And there I saw the world.

Kafka. Hegel. Aristotle. Dog-eared Plath. First editions of Marquez.

I felt like Belle from Beauty and the Beast, being led to the prince's massive library. Would he let me borrow something from here? Or did he keep them to himself?

'This is… beautiful,' I whisper, transfixed. He's watching me watch the bookshelves.

'Pick anything. They're all yours.'

'Really?'

'Really.'

That's when I wonder what such a well-read man is doing in a rural village. If he wanted to he could go anywhere. Reach any height. And yet he chose this simplicity. That day it wasn't just the library that caught my attention. It was his fear. I know there's something stopping him from packing his bags and running away. And it's threatening him.

*

I watch him from my window and I know his shadow is staring back at me. My heart is frenzied with fits. I am walking on wildfire. I am burning in my own fire. And suddenly I don't see him anymore. The porch light comes on. He has left the house and he is walking...

Towards me.

I turn around to meet him and the lights go out.

Panic grips me. Leaking into me like an open pipe. I can smell the fear on me. And whatever is in the room can smell it too. There is a prayer on my lips, but it is so inaudible. Whatever is here is here for me. To scare me out of my house. And out of this village.

Maybe the village ghosts do not want me around, asking questions about the dead. Ghosts?

Too much has happened now for me to not believe.

I try to make my way through the dark. Somewhere in between I find the knob for the utility drawer and pull it open. Grabbing the matchbox inside it I run towards the prayer room. I bump into so many chairs and tables on my way. Ajja was the headmaster of a local school, but I do wish he didn't have so many tables, so many pens and papers and all sorts of odd things lying around. My hair stands on end, my blood cold, goose pimples running along me like tracks. I feel like someone's touching me from everywhere, but it could just be in my head. I finally get to the prayer room and pour the oil into the lamp.

Just as I light the match I hear a voice behind me.

Akka, chooru enne kolpera. Sister, could you please give me some oil?

The matchstick falls from my hands.

I scream.

The next thing I know the lights are back on and there is something lying right in front of me.

The very same body of the boy.

It sends me into a cold sweat. I'm horror struck, a cripple inside my own house.

He suddenly jerks up and his eyes are wide open. He doesn't even blink. I'm still screaming and crying as he chants. *Vetala. Vetala. Vetala.*

I want your blood.

Now, now, now!

By then, the door is kicked open and I can hear footsteps running towards me. The little boy stops laughing and falls to the floor. There's a loud scream coming from outside now and wolves are howling again. I'm shaking so bad. Beads of sweat salt my forehead.

'Are you okay, Noor?'

Kalki is crouching in front of me. He hooks his hands under my arms and pulls me up.

'Yes. Yes, I think I am,' I breathe. My heart is still pounding. He carries me into Ajja's room and sits me on his lap.

'Come back to my place. I don't want you staying here.'

'You came here. You said you wouldn't, but you did.'

'Noor,' he says, tilting my chin. 'I don't think your

grandfather would have wanted me to watch you get hurt and not do a thing about it.'

'Thank you for coming.' It is a faint whisper.

'This can't happen again,' he says. 'Noor, why are you even staying here?'

'Where else could I go? This is my only home here.'

'You can go home,' he says after a long thought.

I'm alarmed. 'As in?'

'Back to Kashmir. Where it is secure and guarded, at least from these ghosts.'

'Are you insane! Are you trying to send me away?'

'No, no.' He holds me as I begin sobbing. 'No, baby. No. I just... I just want you to be safe. And happy. I can't stand to see you get hurt.'

'Then don't ever say that again.'

'Come with me, a little hookah will put you at rest. Maybe I can show you something interesting after.'

'I don't want to see anything interesting! I want to know what killed Kirti and I want to know what's threatening you!'

He doesn't say anything. For a long while we stay there, a tangled mess, a pair of shoelaces tied too tight, and then, he releases me. 'Trust me. Just come.'

Sighing I follow him out of my house. His place is just a small walk away and his door is hanging open from him running out to see me. When we enter I take in the sepia light and close my eyes for a while. I am glad to be back here. I turn my face away from the haunted well outside and walk in.

'What do you want to show me?' I ask.

'It's called astral projection,' he tells me. 'It has happened before naturally and sometimes it is induced by drugs like *bhang* during overdose. And I can do it with hookah. For someone like you, who has never had an out of body experience, you'll need a pill.'

'Is it scary?'

He looks at me skeptically. By now I shouldn't be asking such a question. I've had enough scares to last me a lifetime and I'm still here, alive. My heart is still beating like a bass drum.

'Do you want to get out of your body and run away with me for a while? I'll help you get back to it in an hour, don't worry.'

I hesitate, a mix of uncertainity and guilt. I haven't found answers to Kirti's death yet, the reason I came here. Should I be going off to fantastical lands then? But it is a fleeting thought. And peering into Kalki's kohl smudged eyes, brimming with the longing to be together in an alternate universe, I want nothing more than to be part of every bit of his being. 'Wouldn't our bodies be easy targets for possession then?' I ask.

He nods. 'Rakteswari will protect us.'

I know who she is now. I've been snooping around and found out that she is the good village ghost, who helps travellers; she is Kalki's left hand. The villagers told me that the two of them were tight, best friends even. It was part of the trade. They'd been friends for a long while now. Sangria silk sari and kohl eyes. Spirit and human. There were no boundaries.

And now I remember the story Kirti had told me when I was eight. How Rakteswari had guarded the family home when her father and brother had been away. Her father was supposed to have asked the servants to check on the house and Kirti and her mother thought he did, because at midnight they'd seen someone sleeping with a heavy blanket on their doorstep. But when Krishna uncle returned home he told them that he'd forgotten to tell the servants to keep guard. How could I not remember this? It didn't ring a bell even when Kalki had said her name that day. I wondered how much my parents had made me forget about Herga when we moved back to Kashmir. Never had they hated a place so much.

'Trust her,' he says. 'We can trust her.'

I nod. It doesn't matter. I trust him and I'll follow him to the grave. 'It's where I go when I need to think.'

I raise my eyebrows.

'The Ganges. All the ashes are laid to rest on its waves. This is where you'll find the apsaras. Aren't you tired of seeing ghosts? Don't you want to see other celestial beings?'

'Are mermaids real too?' I ask him dumbly.

He laughs. 'Come on, let's strip down to our souls.'

I wonder if we are going to make love underwater, not our naked bodies but our bare souls; wild sprites on river mouths joining in unison and forming an unbreakable bond. The universe is indeed mysterious.

I am excited now. I allow him to drop the pill into my mouth and take a few drags of his hookah, he closes his eyes and I can see faded lines of tiredness around them. He wears dark circles like glass bangles under his eyes and I swear they are nothing short of a miracle.

My eyes close too, and I begin to step into a world

I have never seen before. It is a third eye opening, a spiritual experience, and no paint or canvas will help me describe it.

Cobalt and azure swirl at the bottom as he drags me down into the water like an anchor. We move down steadfast, windmills of bubbles beading into my hair like crystals. I am water, lush and life giving, and he is water, roaring feral and savage, taking life like a tsunami, a wolfish sea storm. He is a paradox, both brutal and kind as he handles me, and we are at the bottom of the river. There is a kingdom of fish and shells. Women sing from a distance, their white saris glowing in the dark like light houses. Long hair, rose gold jewellery in the heart of teal and sapphire crystals. He leads me away from them and into a small cave.

I see our bodies sitting on the couch, eyes closed, fast asleep.

And then, I see her, Rakteswari.

She is in chiffon and lace, her face a mask, her hair overflowing buttermilk and porcelain. She is so close and yet untouchable. She is watching our bodies and waiting for us to come back. I want to say thank you, and there are so many things I want to say to him, but I don't know how. I am awake in a dream, so wide awake that I begin to swallow it as truth. Her eyes are oat, sandcastles of Tuscan sun, a breath of dandelion.

Her skin is bronze, a rush of glorious cider, and her poise is powerful. I am grateful for her being.

He pulls me away now.

He is looking at me like none of those beautiful damsels, ghosts and half goddesses out there matter to his world. He only sees me, and he sees me with an intensity that frightens me and yet attracts me. I am a hopeless moth to not just a single flame but a forest fire. His love is untameable and nothing can come close to comparison. The horizon tries, I think, remembering an Arctic Monkeys song. It plays in my head like a background score as I dive down further.

His hands slither under my shirt and pull me towards him. I'm all undone again and I'm feeling weightless. My hands turn kryptonite to the contours of his graphite skin. My wet hair spreads behind my head and he coils his fingers into it, his obsidian and soot eyes never once exposed to shutdowns. We can't let this moment go, not now, not ever. When he kisses me there is no water or land. He's soft blankets and cabins and open windows to the sea. It's just the two of us now, bodiless, breathing each other and feeling so helplessly out of control that we can't do anything but give in. I come undone as he glides over every mole on my body, every jutting bone. I know I can't fight this, it's not in me to fight something so phenomenal and unparalleled. I lie on the riverbed, glazing into his eyes, asking him to take me. As he comes down on his knees, his soft smile tickling every inch of me, I gush. I am the river. Even four hundred miles off the coast of his cinnamon paint skin I know I will swim back like an ark with its sail on fire, sweeping away tide and current; bow, hull and mast trickling his name.

Bursts of candyfloss crowd my mouth, sugar coating my senses, playing dangerous games. Pearls line down my throat, sucking in the sweetness of his scent. I cannot bear this, I'm going so terribly insane. I look up at him inquisitively. I can't speak, I realize, but in my head I'm asking all the right questions.

Do you love me enough to hold on?

He nods. Yes, I hear and I smile. Speech is irrelevant and powerless. Silence is an art. We bring ourselves together and say things words could never dream of saying. So this is how it goes. This is how I die. There is no going back now, he is the only one I want.

I dig graves for my sins in his skin, my fingers ploughing his bare back. For a fleeting moment we lock eyes, slicing time into fragile halves. If ever there is a heaven, may it be as beautiful and eternal as this, I think.

And then, he pulls me down, straight into hell, and back onto the couch at home.

Chapter Fourteen

'What's so funny?' I ask him.

'Nothing,' he says. 'I'm just remembering the book I was reading when you came to meet me after the *kola*. You wanted to know about Sisyphus, and I gave you such a vague answer.'

'What's he got to do with us?' I ask, surprised. I'd forgotten about it completely.

'Everything,' he says. 'It is a philosophy of the absurd. About man's futile search for meaning in the face of an unintelligible world devoid of truths, values and god.'

There he goes again, retreating into his own universe of borderline insanity. A place I can't follow him into.

I smile. ‘I’m not an existentialist. Or a nihilist. I love life, I love this world and I love you.’

‘Exactly,’ he replies. ‘When I was reading Camus I agreed with him. But not anymore. I’ve seen you, Noor, and you are the meaning that I’ve been looking for all my life. It’s not futile, my purpose is to love you, to be in love with you. Does that sound silly? Is it so unmanly and threatening to our machoism to be sensitive and compassionate? That’s what’s wrong with most of these philosophers. They spurn god, they spurn love, they spurn life. And life is nothing without love and god. And when I say god why can it not mean anything and everything at all? Who is asking us to define everything that we see and don’t see? God can be nothing and god can be everything. We make our own gods and we become our own gods. In *seva*. In doing good and being good.’

He is right about that, I admit. There is no limit to what we can become, whether this is positive or negative. The human soul is that vast, that infinite. And only love can be plentiful enough to fill up that soul space. And they don’t understand that without love, there is no meaning to life. If not love then what? What can save us?

I hug him tight as we keep on. *We save each other.*

We are walking towards the *bhoota* temple next to my Ajja’s house. He is holding my hand and I am still shaken, in a pleasant manner, from the experience of bodiless movement. 'I felt so alive, and at the same time I didn't know if I even existed,' I muse.

'Don't worry. It's impossible to doubt your existence,' he says to me. 'Or at least, Descartes seems to think so.'

'Now who's that? Another one of your great philosophers?'

He chuckles. 'He's great, of course. He said that the mind is distinct from the body. He argued about the possibility of minds or souls existing without bodies. Because bodies are extended.'

'Is that how we could do it?'

'Perhaps.'

'What was that pill you gave me?'

He winks at me. 'Secret.'

And just as I am about to retort I get a call. It is Baba. I walk away from Kalki and answer it. It's been a few weeks since he's called. Not that they call every day, but with the current situation I'd expected them to keep me updated.

'Baba? I called you so many times! Why didn't it once get through?'

Baba is delirious, he is saying many things at once. I can't hear anything, but I feel tensed already. Something is not right.

'They've burned down the house,' Baba cries. I can hear his sobs and they blaze into me like a cannonball. 'Don't come back any time soon, Noor *beta*.'

Grief slides like ice down my back. I close my eyes and sway. My house, my Baba's favourite easy chair, my mother's cherished kitchen. All the precious things I've ever known. Daadi's face swims into focus as I blink back tears. Where will they stay now? Of course they have friends to shelter them. But who will cover for the losses? Who will give us asylum forever?

I fall to the ground and I can hear Kalki running towards me.

'Hey! What's wrong?!'

I'm weeping now, and I'm loose, from my undone hair to my shaking limbs, my quivering mouth to my spilling eyes. 'Oh god, no! What am I even doing here? I can't, I can't! I feel so guilty…'

He's holding me now, but there is nothing he can do to ease the pain. He tries to get me into the house, but a few villagers have already seen us and I look like someone died.

*

He fixes me a cup of coffee, black and sugarless, and I accept it with grateful hands.

He sits across the bed and looks straight into me like reading a book. I feel overexposed and small.

'Whenever you're ready,' he says.

I take a deep breath and inhale the aroma of the drink. The warm blankets make me feel better now. It has started raining again and the clouds are a shade of porpoise. 'My… my family home has been destroyed. In Kashmir.'

'How?' He is as baffled as I am.

'Someone burned it… they haven't found out who… I don't think they ever will.'

I suddenly rise from the bed. I am angry now. 'What is this! What did we even do? And I feel so helpless sitting here doing nothing. I want to go back.'

'Do you?' he asks quietly.

'Baba won't let me. He doesn't think it's safe anymore.'

'He is right. It isn't.'

I dismiss his statement with a wave of my hand. Frustration buries itself in my brows and I am pacing the ground now. 'Is there anything that can be done about this? I mean…' I look at him and I am struck by the most deviant of ideas. I don't know what overcomes me when I say, 'you said something about cursing people. Rivalries. Is it… it's possible to put curses on people we hate, isn't it?'

He's scandalized. 'Noor, that is not my kind of magic. I don't touch that. It is evil.'

I scoff. Everything he is playing with is evil anyway, it is black magic. 'Your father and his father did it.'

'I am not my father,' he says stiffly. He shakes his head. 'Noor, you're not being rational. You need to just take some time and think clearly. You are obviously traumatized. They destroyed your house and you family probably doesn't have a roof to live under. And if they do they're still hurt and terrified. I get it, you are worried. But it's wrong to use magic to hurt people.'

'But we are hurting bad people, Kalki,' I interject, but he has made up his mind. I know he won't help me and a part of me doesn't want him to help me. I know I'm behaving impulsively. I know tomorrow I'll be mortified about what I've been even thinking.

'Magic requires a lot of responsibility,' he says to me, almost in an inaudible whisper, almost as if he is speaking to himself. 'Never give a sword to a man who can't dance,' he reminds me.

I rub my eyes. 'I'm sorry. I got carried away.'

He moves closer and hugs me. 'You're going to be fine. Your family is going to be fine. And even Kashmir is going to be fine.'

But you aren't, I think.

And I don't have to say it. He knows it too. He's still looped his arms over me and he's gazing into me like a daydream.

'I know it's hard. I'm sorry we're all so helpless,' he says, looking down, a little ashamed.

'Bad things happen and we can't do anything about them. Women are raped, lovers are killed in the name of honour, friends are backstabbed in the fight for power. As humans we're a doomed race, aren't we?' He shakes his head sadly. 'I don't know what else to say. Here's to hoping some of us survive the wars we create and save our humanity. Here's to hoping there won't be anymore Kashmirs or Syrias and children who grow up knowing only battle scars. There will be peace one day, Noor, but you must be patient. Rebuilding can happen only from the aftermath. Pain will give birth to empathy. Until then, we are all selfish, worthless. Until then, none of us give a damn about one another.

But there will come a time when we all realize we need to put our weapons down and kill only the monsters within us. And if we can, save the gods. The goodness. The mercy. The tender heartedness. The humanity.'

Long live, I think to myself.

That's all I can say. For myself. For us. For mankind.

'May we forgive ourselves our madness and hope for a better world and order,' he says to me.

I don't have the heart to bring up bad governments and a civilization built entirely on religion and politics. I nod quietly, my mind cartwheeling back to my home.

Everything goes down in flames some day. Everything.

Chapter Fifteen

It's been two weeks since the incident and I get the news that Baba is staying with our family friend and his wife. They have started looking for a place to rent, but they are still greatly affected by the loss.

I've told them many times that I want to come back. But even Daadi said to me, *Noor beta, I am glad you ran away. Even though I was angry at you initially. Allah has seen to it to protect you from all of this.*

The only thing keeping me sane from all the madness back home is a certain kohl eyed man with earrings and cryptic tattoos. Ebony and noir whip into his eyes like reservoirs, and in that infinite juncture I am susceptible to drowning. How did he do it? How did he have me walking straight into his arms? How did he blur out every other face I'd ever known? He is my bad habit, my Achilles heel and personal hell. He's turned me into one of those water nymphs, but I'm the only one who's discovered Atlantis. It's all so ironic. Look at me, I think, some rich London artist running around selling paintings and coming home to a war wrecked state. Look at me, finding my way to a daredevil, an intoxicated god. Of all the lethal things that he could have done to me, loving me was the worst. Because it made me love him back.

And I don't know which is worse — seeing him in my dreams or seeing him in my reality. He is a phantom of the mind.

'You're a ghost too, Noor. Look at you, always haunting me in my sleep,' he says, jumping into bed. I look at him, eyes wide, and he laughs.

'How do you do that?' I ask him.

'Do what?' he asks, mischief shrouding his tone.

'Never mind. You're not going to tell me anything anyway. How can I love you if I know nothing about you?'

'You love me?' Another mischievous twinkle in his pitch black eyes.

I nod seriously. 'I came here to find my best friend. I couldn't accept that she was dead. I found you; and God, you were so alive it hurt. But Kalki,' I said, looking into his eyes, 'I wish I'd known you sooner. You're my best friend too.'

His eyes are moist. 'Really?'

I nod. 'Really. I'm glad you texted me from Kirti's number. I know it's crazy, but it was serendipitous. I was brought here only and only to love you. Now I know.'

'I never even let myself dream… of this.' He holds my hands tightly, my palms facing upward. 'I couldn't.'

'I want you to. You deserve more than you think you do, Kalki. All the breaths I have ever taken to keep me alive were only taken to lead me to you so that we could be here, stay here, in this moment of infinite beauty. Growing up here, my friendship with Kirti, going away to learn of the arts you understand through your philosophers and coming back now in search of answers. Every path I've walked has been bringing me to you. You are my answer. I was born for you.'

He looks at me, so grateful, so full of disbelief, and he cups my face. 'I could die for you,' he says and bites into my lip.

*

Two days later we're rested on a river bank, our hair kissed by a light breeze, roof to sand and dust as we dip our ankles in the water. The sky is a fishbowl filled with swishing airplanes and he's throwing his clothes off like the dust jacket of a classic novel. The wind hits his bare back and I run my fingers over it, watching how the goosebumps bloom like fresh springs. Not all rivers in Herga have names. This one is just another village waterway that nobody visits. But it feels like our spot, even though I don't dare dream about something like that.

'Once I leave London I'm going to settle here,' I tell him.

'It's a dangerous place for you.'

'Don't you want me to be here? With you?'

'I do.'

But then, he doesn't say anything more and that frightens me. I tug his sleeve and he looks at me with such a sad face, I can't help but ask him what's wrong.

'I'm so happy, Noor.'

'Isn't that a good thing?'

'I don't know. I'm not used to it. This happiness.'

He has wrenched my heart out with that one statement. I hold his hand tighter and look around. I'm glad this place is isolated. I pull his face towards me and kiss him. 'You deserve all the happiness in the world and more. And I've told you this before and I'll tell you this again.'

'But not you. I don't deserve you.'

I punch him in the arm. 'Stop saying these things. Where is all this coming from?'

'I'm just scared this will come to an end one day. It's so special to me, Noor. I don't ever want it to go away.'

I squeeze his arm and rest my head on his shoulder. 'Trust me, it won't.' I look at him, a new idea dawning on me. 'What if we both run away to London? I'm sure you could get into a good college, especially with the kind of brains you've got there.' I knock his head and he chuckles.

'I can't come to London. I can't move out of here.'

'What do you mean? What's holding you back?'

'My family,' he says.

'Your family is dead, Kalki,' I reply gently.

'No, you don't understand.'

'Make me understand.'

The water is touching our toes now. The clouds have turned grey and so has his mood.

'I don't want to leave. That's all.'

'But you want to, right?'

'No. I want to stay here and die here. This is where I belong. In this madness,' he heaves. 'Besides, what do I do in a place like Europe? I'm sure it's beautiful, but it's got its own darkness.'

'What do you mean?'

'The Western world? The one all our Indian cities are trying to imitate? You think it is so great?'

I don't say anything. I don't know where this is going.

'Shit,' he curses loudly and takes a few steps into the water. I read his foot prints like tea leaves in a cup, running mine over them and coming up behind him.

'I don't want to live in the city.'

'But why?'

'I… I like the quiet life. I like living slow.'

'We can… we'll just get a nice, cosy house with heating, snuggle near the fireplace with our socks on, read books and stuff. Isn't that quiet and slow enough?

I don't believe you when you say you don't want to leave. Give me a better reason, because this one's downright lousy.'

'I've got way too many reasons, Noor,' he says, defensive. 'What's so great about cities anyway? What's making us go so rotten? What is wrong with our generation? Why are we so obsessed with money and power and sex and drugs and getting our way with everything? Why can't we just want food and love. That's all we should be wanting. That's all we need.'

'Wow,' I say angrily. 'For someone so intellectual you're being very judgemental right now.'

'Noor, that's not what I…' He rubs his forehead. 'Okay, I take that back. I lost my shit. Listen, don't push me with this. I'm bound to stay. I can't tell you. It's complicated.'

I hug him from behind. He doesn't move. 'When you're ready.'

'I might never be.'

'I'm going to wait anyway.'

'I love you,' he says flatly.

'I love you too.'

Chapter Sixteen

He is my favourite monster. Werewolf to my wild moonlight. Lotus to my forbidden waters. Born of half gods and animals. Light to my dark, darkness to my light. His name is a song on my lips, a poem of wonders seeping right into my bones, and it moves me, shakes me, terrifies me. Burns me, kills me, revives me.

I saw a dream I couldn't undo. It started out as a poem and ended in an epitaph. I followed a love child of deserts and summer rains into a deep well that chained me to its ground. And there I saw my best friend's ghost. I wanted to ask her so many things, like why she left me stranded, but I was so happy to see her. I put it behind me and hugged her.

When I wake up the same pair of eyes stare back at me. Just that these belong to a man.

'You were dreaming about her.'

Don't you ever?'

'Always.'

'Do you remember her as I do? As the most engaging friend, so very delightful and good-natured. She shared everything with me. Pencils, hair bows, secrets. I'll never find another friend like her again,' I confess, feeling a little empty.

'I remember her as a baby. I watched my mother give birth to her. God, she was so tiny. I saw her and I thought, something as fragile as that should never have a father… like him. Kirti was ill-fated. Right from the start. We all were. All I know now is I'll never have a sister like her again. I remember it all like it was just yesterday.'

So do I. And I don't remember her as someone who'd kill herself. Or even someone who'd dabble with the other side to talk to her dead mother. Kirti liked to stay out of it all. I try to shut out everything the villagers ever told me, but doubt still clings onto me like handcuffs. 'Did she seem troubled?'

He shakes his head, just as confused. 'Not even a bit. Even on the last day she was smiling. I had no clue.'

I want to protect him from his loss. I know he wishes they were there. He thinks he can fool me with his devil-may-care attitude, but I know he's hurting on the inside. I know he misses his family, no matter how fragmented it was.

'You can visit the same dream a million times and still not realize it is a dream,' he says wistfully. I watch the magic unfold within the fissures of his wounds. He is a flash of orb emerging from the grip of his past; he was almost killed once, but he slipped into metamorphosis and conquered death. He's probably blocked out every image of his old life and turned his memories into holocausts. I don't know if I should feel pity or fear. So instead I just love him endlessly, because that's all I can do for him.

I'm worried that this source of wound has no end to it. We belong to the same scars, it is her. She wrote me letters and hung pots of sweetness on her head. Her skirts were long and flowed like the wind, her hair a shot of silver dust, a smooth layout of braided perfection. She was a child, and yet her eyes carried so much maturity in a world that couldn't grow up as fast as she did. And then, they had to take her. Whoever they were, they had to take her.

'It must have hurt so bad,' I whisper, touching his jade tendrils and pushing them behind his ears. 'Losing your family to black magic.'

He looks up at the ceiling and a small tear escapes his eye. I don't know what to do. This sudden revelation of emotion has me stumped. I move closer and put my arm around his torso. 'Kalki, you never spoke to anyone. About it, I mean.'

'No. Nobody would understand how I felt.'

'I do.'

He takes a deep breath. 'She died and my lungs gave out. You know that feeling when your heart sinks into the pit of your stomach? I let it stay there and rot. I wanted it gone. I switched off. I loved her. I loved my sister. Wherever she is, I need to know she's okay.'

And we lie there like that, in nirvana, for what seems like a butterfly's half life, and then, he says to me, 'I grew up hating that well. I'll do anything to close it. It took my mother and my sister away.'

My mouth falls open. Has he changed his mind now or is this just a sudden revelation? 'Did you just say you hate the well?'

He looks away, 'I try not to.'

I don't want to rub it in his face, so I don't prod further about his contradictory statement. There's no time for I-told-you-so's. We need solutions fast.

'Why can't you close it then? Or why can't you just move out of this place?' I repeat.

He closes himself to me again and drifts back into that space I can never reach out to. He gets up and pulls out his favourite apparatus. I pull the bed sheet towards me and watch him take a drag. He looks peaceful now and I can only hope there will come a time when he doesn't need smoke to help his heart be serene. Look at those spider eyes, I think, as he sits there with his hookah, pan and kiwi, hot coal and raven ash. How is he to me more beautiful than art?

'I can't,' he says. 'I'm bound to all of it.'

'Why can't you do anything about that sick well?'

'Because…'

He's stopped in his tracks. I know he's already said too much.

'Because what?' I ask him, impatient.

'I…'

'Say it, Kalki. Say it, I won't let a word out of this place.' I want him to trust me. I don't understand why he doesn't.

'When…' he stammers. I grip his hands and move my thumbs over his palms. He continues, his gaze, calculative. 'When the well was made, someone buried a sack of garlic, chilli and special herbs in it. Well, not just someone. My great grandfather, or maybe an ancestor even older. But the point is, it wasn't just any random pouch. My family has been practicing black magic for generations now. It was a bag that had a lot of special powers and my great grandfather created it to destroy this whole village. He wanted to wipe out all the crops and fields and women and children and turn this place into a ghost town.'

It takes a while to sink in. 'Why would… why would your ancestors do that?'

He shrugs. 'They were just malicious. Evil doesn't necessarily need intent. Maybe someone commissioned them to do it. Maybe they were just bitter men who sought out to destroy good people. Whatever it was, it stayed through generations.'

I close my eyes. My tongue is numb. 'This is all just crazy. Do you want me to believe all of this? Do you believe what you've seen so far?'

I don't think I have an answer for that. Instead I say, 'So what stopped him from destroying Herga?'

'Rakteswari, protector of the living dead.' He takes a deep breath. Imaginary friend, I want to refute, but I've seen her too. Ink locks and gingerbread face. 'She put a curse on the family for inviting bad spirits into Herga. And we have been doomed ever since.'

'But she is your friend.'

'No.'

'No?' I repeat after him, shocked.

'So everything that you said... about her protecting us...is a lie?'

His laugh is mirthless. 'Oh, she will protect me. And she'll protect you too, just because I ask her to. It's a deal of sorts.'

'I don't understand.'

'Simple. She wants something. Until she gets it from me I can't die.'

'So... you're not friends?' I ask, aghast.

'She was Kirti's friend. And even our mother's. They were so innocent and she led them into that godforsaken well.'

'What do you mean?'

My heart is skipping beats like frogs leaping onto rocks. I'm going to find out. I'm going to know the whole story, the puzzle pieces are finally going to fit.

I came here for this. I've waited so long for this.

And all of a sudden I feel like I'm not ready.

'She lured them,' he says bitterly. 'She lured them into jumping in, using them to dig the sack out. Rakteswari's powers are dying. She can't hold the black magic over the village off for too long, the sack is making her weak. One day or the other, this place is going to be in ruins. With all my powers there is nothing I can do to save it. Until that sack is removed from the well and taken elsewhere, nothing can be done.'

Now it makes sense. 'So that's why the well can't be sealed. Because that would mean locking the sack into it forever and making it inaccessible.' Until now my issues with the well were purely psychological. My best friend and her mother had jumped into it and ended their lives. I couldn't imagine why anybody wouldn't want to close it after all that it has done. My personal hatred would have done it the minute I saw it. But now I knew the consequences and now I knew how torn Kalki was between keeping it there and shutting it down.

'Why is she loyal to you then? Why did she protect our bodies when we astro projected?'

'Because she needs me and my… powers. To keep the village safe from my ancestors' hex. Together we're more powerful, she and I. We buy the village more time.'

'Is… is this why you can't leave this place?'

He shakes his head. 'It's a family curse. I'm bound to it. I don't know what will happen to me if I leave. Call us superstitious but nobody in my family has even tried to leave.'

I don't want to think about what could happen. I walk towards him and put my arms around him. I want to tell him I'm sorry, but me being sorry is not going to help.

It's not just his family that's doomed.

Our love was doomed right from the start. But that's not even the sad part. It's that I've always known.

I've always known we were aircrashes. The kind that couldn't retrieve even its black box to be honest. I've known; and just like Kirti's death, I've failed to accept the truth.

What does that say about me?

Chapter Seventeen

I'd stay back just for the sunset from this window. I like the way the curtain falls over its face, like silky hair. This is where he watches me. I still remember that first day when I saw him here, looking right at me, probably wondering why my Ajja's house wasn't empty anymore.

Time undresses itself in front of me like a stripper. The clothes fall off one by one and she tells me she has to leave now. Her shift is over. There's nothing left here anymore except emptiness.

Wool ferns of alabaster cloud dot the horizon. Thirty miles of sand dollar sky. An elaborate pineapple sun. His silhouette adorns the walls, dancing to the light.

As he looks into my eyes he tells me a secret, 'You look at me and, god, does the universe stop breathing.'

I've a wide smile. We are having coffee, scented with the happiness we are wearing. Garlands of desire. And yet I feel a strange tugging within. What if this doesn't last? What if my joy is otherworldly. This is surely an imbalance. I am too happy, and this kind of happiness is too easily taken away.

The sun is melted wax to a golden river. Rain is a swift seductress yet again, enticing stubborn clouds and coaxing the sky to let her fall. The gods are good to us. The heat is kept calm inside Pandora's box and the rain is mild and duty bound to not hurt us too much. He is sitting in the armchair beside me, smoking and caught up with his own thoughts, and I am looking into my own mind, wondering what will happen of us. I never saw this coming. I never did.

And just as I doze off I see him.

A man, appearing out of nowhere.

I jolt and Kalki rises from his chair slowly, his face grave.

The man is a wreck. Perspiration drools on his forehead and his face is contorted with pain and fear. I feel Kalki stiffen beside me. He dashes forward and holds the frightened man in his arms.

'Jaado aanu?' What's wrong?

'Olai barkana?' Please, can I come in?

Yes. Of course.

He begins his story after Kalki settles him down with a cup of tea. His voice quivers.

'I was going back home on my bike,' he says.

And I was a little drunk, but still conscious. And out of the blue I see a woman in a white sari. I know she is a yakshi even though I haven't seen one my entire life, I just know she is. Because it was late at night and nobody was around, and she suddenly jumps out of the forest and disappears when I pull my brakes.

'Bethu jaadaanu?' Kalki asks. *What happened next?*

There are rivulets of curiosity on his face, tunnels of seriousness booming into him like trains running through them, trains of thought. I want to know what he's thinking, what he's already figured out from the man's tale, but I don't want to interrupt him.

'Bethu...' And then.

'I start my engine and begin to ride my bike again, but I know something is wrong,' he says. 'So I check my mirror, and she is there, right behind me on the passenger seat, sitting as if nothing's wrong, as if it is so natural of her to be sitting there. I don't look back at all. I ride all the way back home, jump out of the vehicle and run into my house. My wife is waiting up for me and when she sees me she screams.'

'*Soole,*' he says. *See this.*

He pulls his shirt up and there are long red gashes all over his flesh. The scarlet scars are like tiger stripes and I gasp. The man looks as terrified as me. I don't think he's still got over the fact that the ghost on the bike ripped into him with her frost blade nails.

'Help me,' he says to Kalki. 'If she kills me who will take care of my wife and daughter?'

Kalki assures him that nobody is going to kill him. Anyway, he's going to give him a special amulet that will protect him. There is nothing to worry about, he says, as he walks him into one of the forbidden rooms of his house, the place where he keeps his wolves. I'm not allowed to go there. It has a lot of things that are magical and powerful, and no normal person can handle the kind of dark magic that a single room possesses.

When Kalki has spoken privately to the terrified man he is a monsoon of praises. He thanks him and tells him how he thought his whole world came to a stand still. Everything was so dark and terrifying.

'No darkness that you encounter should ever be allowed a space inside your body. No darkness should ever be greater than the light you hold within you,' Kalki says.

The man bows and he dismisses him. When he is gone he comes back to me. I wonder how there is so much toxicity around us and we still never lose hope. Hope is fragile, like ego, like the heart. But it is still alive in all of us, as a curse, as a blessing. It keeps us going forward, but it also aligns us always from reality. And as far as this beautiful man is concerned, all I have is hope. Hope is what is keeping me here, in this little village, even when I am so scared.

*

That night we are in bed, the curtains drawn, and we look eye to eye. We are speaking, and our spoken word is mind language. I finally break the silence and tell him, 'You are very brave. To be helping people like this. Even if it means putting your life at risk.'

He laughs, but it doesn't meet his eyes. It is cold, aloof. Tired even. 'Sometimes I just want to leave and never look back. Start over. But wherever I go, this life will come after me. I'm linked, chained to two worlds, and there is nothing I can do about it.'

'You are Kalki. *Called* Kalki. The name of a powerful god.'

'I am Kalki to my family. The last of the Vishnu

avatar, the destroyer, the one who ends everything. When they made my horoscope they said I was going to be the downfall of my fathers, and they wanted to kill me. But my mother protected me and convinced them to tie this amulet around me.' He raises his left hand and I see a silver bracelet dangling from his wrist. 'It nullifies the prophecy, or so they say. I wish it didn't, I wish I was the last of our wretched kind. And I can't take it off, because my father has made me promise not to.'

'But your father is dead!' I exclaim. And then, I realize my fallacy.

'I don't know. Physically, yes. The remains of his body are in the Ganga. But I hope he's burning in Hell, I really do.'

What's holding him back? I wonder again, and for the first time this question feels heavier than the question of Kirti's suicide. Why doesn't he leave? Why doesn't he tell Rakteswari that he wants out of it? Sure she wants his power to help her undo the powers of the sack in the well, but can't he just run away? Or would she come after him?

It hits me. Guilt. He thinks they deserve it. For all that his ancestors have done to the people of Herga, for all the curses they've cast on their families, he is repenting and paying. He has no other choice but to stay and help the woman who talked his mother and sister into killing themselves.

I feel so worried for him. And there is nothing I can do. Feeling helpless, I touch his cheek and say, 'You consume me. Fiercely. Maddeningly.' He doesn't say anything, so I continue.

'I told the stars about you. And I swear they were jealous.'

He smiles. It is a smile of acceptance.

Like there is nothing we can do to save ourselves.

We have already jumped.

Chapter Eighteen

The night we fall out of fashion, he is sitting in his chair sipping on red wine, his eyes the colour of the universe, stars floating like lotus leaves on a pool of pitch black night. They wouldn't like sad boys, his Amma said. You're going to have to hide it with flashlight smiles and rosemary cheeks. I watch him wreak havoc to himself, eclipsing his heart, trying to burn his feelings down. He stays quiet, not because he has nothing to say but because nothing can be said, for who would understand anyhow. To me, though, just as I heard it for the very first time to the now, his voice is music to flame lilies. Fire engine red, blooming to his command alone. He is a terrifying single tenant looming within the unpaid rent of himself, with magic for handcuffs. He is proud of his singularity. He is alone and he is alien. But he is true and he is special and he is unapologetic in his uniqueness. His loneliness is an acquired skill. They said he once broke his bones to accommodate his soul, it couldn't be confined within himself. They said he ripped his heart to accommodate lovers but it overflowed and tore apart. He is a castle that once had open gates but is now locked with metal chains. And I know, deep in my heart, I love him so damn much.

I love him, but something tells me it is too late. I want to go back in time and change everything. We'll love as children, in the most honest and blameless of ways. We will grow up together, away from this pain.

But that is all in another time. Because we are here and we are unwell. We are here, in a place that has chained us down and done unto us open heart surgery.

Love is work, I realize. Sometimes we're in sync and sometimes we're two hammers. I don't know how to console him, the feeling of dread is so heavy on our hearts, I feel sick.

And now we are fighting again, and we are in bed.

The rain only gets worse. We don't go out and it kills us. He doesn't let me go to Ajja's house. I don't want to, because of what happened with the corpse of the young boy. But we're arguing again, about so many things.

Like how he should close the well.

Like what's going to happen when I go back to London.

He says my family will never accept him. I say I don't care. He kisses me and I forget the rest of the world.

'How long do you think I'll keep you here?' he asks me. 'Forever? Forever is a joke, Noor. I can't get out of this place and you'll be miserable here.'

I lie on his chest and whisper, 'What's misery if I've got you?'

'Noor…'

'I can stay here, I don't mind. I just need to go to Kashmir in between to see my family. And definitely for the house warming. Baba says they've found a new house.'

He narrows his eyes. 'Does your baba know about us?'

'I'll tell him when I go back this time. I'll tell him I'm going to be staying here now.'

He is bound by vulnerability. 'But I can't do that

to you, Noor. We both know this is not your world. And it's not right or safe keeping you here. What if something happens to you because of me? I couldn't bear it.'

'Hmm.' I'm running my hands all over him, but he pushes me away. 'Why didn't you think of this earlier?'

'I don't know. I saw you and I didn't think about anything else.'

'Don't think about anything else. Except this,' I say and pull his jaw closer and crush my lips onto his. He's not listening. He kisses me for a while, but I can tell he's distracted. Worry is distracting him. He slowly lifts me up and places me between the two pillows. Kissing my forehead he puts a shirt on and walks into the other room where the hookah is.

I'm irked. I walk out of the bedroom and look for him.

He's sitting in the veranda, smoking and staring at the empty sky. He looks like a child, his face so confused, so undecided. He's changed so much for me, I know, but why can't he change just a little bit more?

I want him to move away from Herga. This place is killing him. London will be good for both of us, I think. Or maybe even Kashmir, after it settles down a bit. Or maybe some nice city like Delhi. Or somewhere south of India, like Kochi or Bangalore.

And as I go back into the room my head full of dreams, leaving him to his hookah, I see someone. I see my best friend.

For the first time in years her face is not a mirage. She is looking right through the window and smiling at me, waving. I remember her as she is. From the fields. From the toothless laughs. From coconut oil hair and flower garlands. From dancing around with long skirts and jumping with the goats. It was all so ethereal.

I can't believe you're here, I want to say. Are you really here?

Her hair, a smooth slide down her face, glistening in the Herga sun. Black tendrils of magnificence. Cusps of silver.

Noor, she says. Her voice is bubbled with excitement. *I miss you. I'm sorry I never replied.*

I want to tell her it's okay. Oh sweet baby. It's all okay now that you're here.

She opens the window for me and I move towards it. *Come.*

'What about Kalki?' I ask. I'm about to turn

around and call him, but she grabs my hand and says, *he never used to play with us. It was just us two, right?*

I want to tell you about this well I've been to, Noor. You should see it, you should come with me. It is the best well in the world.

No, Kirti, I say. This feels wrong. I think you should just stay with me in this room. Let's talk. Let me make some chai for you. You look like you've been out in the cold even when it's burning forty degrees right now. Talk to me. How have you been? I love you.

She looks irritated. *You've always been such a scaredy cat. You never wanted to do anything out of the ordinary. Colour outside the lines. It's fun to be a little messed up, a little less uptight. Loosen up a little.* She winks at me. *You've already done that with my brother. Now look at the other things. Rebel a bit. Throw that old shawl out and let's go roll in the mud. Write on the trees. Jump in the well. You can't always be like this, Noor. You need to come out, know the excitement and live life. You need to live life, Noor, when you're alive. Or else, it'll pass by and you'll regret not doing things.*

I can't comprehend what she's saying, but it still makes sense. My head is hurting. I feel dizzy, but I nod.

'Yes.'

I climb out of the window and her hand never lets go. It pricks me like sugared thorn. It is sweet and yet it is danger. I am a lamb as I follow her out, and together, hand in hand, we walk towards the well.

There is so much happening around me, so much dancing, so much of fairy lights and baubles and fireworks. Everything is white and I am floating. Nothing matters except finding her. There is so much to say, so much of catching up to do.

I see just the tip of a red sari. I follow it. Music pours into my ears and I'm suddenly entranced.

Chapter Nineteen

I look inside the well. *Noor! This place is so cool,* Kirti says. Her mother is standing right next to her and her arms are wide open. *Noor, bale, laippula de. Noor, daughter, why don't you jump?*

She is wearing broken bangles and they're cutting into her wrist. White flowers settle on her long tresses as she calls out my name. I smile and wave at them. I am so happy to see them.

They're waving back. All of them.

Come on in, Kirti says. *This is where we live now. That house was getting old anyway. We can all look after Kalki from down here, he can live a peaceful life if we help him fulfil his life's purpose.*

I pull up my skirt and put my leg over the stone. There is a woman in a red sari standing next to me. It is her again. She is pale like the moon and she is closing up on me. Her hands outstretched, it looks like she's about to push me. She is still smiling, still malicious, and for a second I realize that I've been trapped.

I look back into the well and Kirti and her mother are both looking up at me expectantly. Her mother looks like Kalki, except that her tresses are long and her eyes are larger. She has her hands held high, like she would catch me if I fall, and in that flash of moment my mind steers back to him. If it was a choice between going back to Kirti and staying with Kalki, what would it be? Whose arms would I fall into first and whose arms would catch me and hold me like a safe locker?

My mind is consumed by guilt. I can feel him inside me, so powerful, and his love so everlasting. How could I even imagine jumping?

No, I cry. Kirti, come out of there.

I am eight again and I am holding her hand and twisting us around. We are spinning, laughing, our hair wild in the wind, slapping against our faces and coursing into our open mouths. We are making mud castles near the river and splashing water on each other. It is running through me, like a film, so unreal, so terribly beautiful, and it is wrecking me. I am crying again. My cheeks glisten tears and I am pressing onto the walls of the well and peering down.

Kirti, please come out. Please.

She is fading now and I can't see anything except water. I reach out, but pull my hand back swiftly. No.

Cold hands drape over my body and I scream. They are pressing me down and I try to push them away. They're all over me now, and a howl digs into my ears. It sounds like a banshee, a woman screaming in pain, and it is overpowering my own cries for help.

'Kalki!'

The hands grow tighter and the women inside the well start laughing and rejoicing. They are dancing and their voices sound like tambourines. There is no more water inside the well and I'm still screaming, screaming so loud, but I don't think anyone can hear me.

'Kalki! KALKI!'

I'm throwing my voice, but nothing has felt so feeble. The hands singe into me and I close my eyes. When I open them again I am facing the well. I am looking right into it. At any moment I might just slip and fall, like it was an accident. And nobody will ever be able to tell that I was pushed.

'Kalki!' I croak feverishly for the last time.

He comes running and the grip unfastens. I turn around and she is fading, and for the first time she isn't smiling. Anger erupts on her brows and she is still desperately trying to hold onto me, but there's something that's stopping her force. He's saying something to her, chanting, and she is trying to shield herself with her hands. I know she's going to come back. I know he's not destroying her, just keeping her away. But her hands are no longer gripping me and I feel relieved. Another pair of arms cover me, masculine ones, firm hands that pull me away from the well.

I've fallen to the ground and I can't stop choking out water. I didn't drown, I didn't even jump, but there is so much in my lungs that I'm coughing up.

'Noor, Noor. Listen to me.' I look up with tired eyes and I see only his face. 'You're okay, but you're going to have to let me lift you up.'

I raise my hands and he takes me. Carrying my limp body he kicks the front door open and saunters in. We are in the bedroom again and we don't say a thing. I am still in shock. I can't believe that a village ghost who was supposed to protect me tried to kill me. Does this mean I am cursed too, like Kirti and her mother? That I can be sacrificed and given away unlike the other villagers of this place? Am I not worth protecting to her?

'What did you do to scare her away?' I ask him, feeling groggy. My head is like clattering pans on the inside and I don't know where all this noise is coming from.

'Nothing,' he says. 'She'll be back.'

My heart is pounding. I saw her eyes, red with rage. She wanted to destroy me in the same way she took Kirti away, for a purpose that is doomed from the very start. The sack is irretrievable, but she will not stop trying, cannot. I'm supposed to feel fear, but now I only feel anger. And then, I look at Kalki and I know what he's thinking. He's plagued with stress.

'It'll be fine, hey.' I rest my hand over his. He takes it back. He is cold and I don't know why.

'I'm sorry, Kalki.'

'I'm sorry too,' he replies.

My eyes are full of sea, my heart full of storm.

'I can't believe this, Noor,' he says.

'Neither can I.'

'No, you don't understand. I'm going to have to do something that's going to… to hurt both of us a lot. But there is no other way.'

'What do you mean?' I ask, my heart rate rising.

He looks down at his licorice palms, unable to meet my gaze. 'Aristotle believed that the goal of life was happiness. He never once said happiness is so short lived, you know.'

I wonder what he means by that, but I don't wonder too hard, because it might mean something horrible. And I'm just not ready to accept it.

If I lose him, who will ever kiss me when my mouth is dripping with last night's coffee and yesterday's secrets? Who will hold me like I am a flower in a rain storm, shelter me like a tree protects the innermost of its baby leaves? Who will touch me like a paroxysmal shower of flames? Who will gun into me like bullets made of petals and feathers? Who will?

I can't lose him. I can't talk to anybody about books, art, culture, life. His mind is filled with my diary entries. He knows the lines of my palm and the moles under my clothes like nobody else. He knows the intricacies and little details like he has studied me in his magic books. And nobody can quote Allen Ginsberg and Katherine Mansfield like he does. He breathes poetry, breathes it into me, and he is my lifeline. All the crooks and gashes and trails on my palms and all the stars that make up forecasts and crystal gazing will tell you this — he belongs with me, to me.

He offers me a drink and I accept graciously. He puts me to bed, and when my head hits the pillow I am already drowsy from the potion he has given me.

'Am I going to astro project again?' I ask dreamily.

'No,' he says curtly. His mouth is a thin line. He is angry. 'You're going to just sleep, baby.' He pulls the sheets over me and turns his face away.

But I have already seen it. The tear that's fallen down his cheek.

I wake up in the early hours of the morning. The room is smaller now, because of the three suitcases near the bed. They're mine. I'd left them in Ajja's house, most things all over the place. I'm sure he's found them all and packed them. I don't even want to ask what they're doing here. As groggy as I am, I know what's on his mind and I just hate it.

I'll do anything I can to stop him from pushing me away. Even if it means risking my life.

'This can't happen again. She can't do this to you too and I can't bear to lose you too.'

I feel like crying. But there are no tears left in me.

'Noor, as long as you are with me, you are cursed.'

'No, Kalki. This is just… it's just superstition.'

'Did you not see what happened to you yesterday?'

'But you saved me!'

He is shaking his head. 'I won't always be around to save you. I couldn't save my sister, I couldn't save my mother. You're part of me, Noor. Not the village, me. It doesn't matter to her if you live or die. With me, death is not far away. You have to go home, Noor. I should have known you weren't safe here.' He is staring at open palms, avoiding my gaze. But I refuse to let this go so easily without a fight.

'Run away with me,' I beg him. 'Bring your wolves. Your hookah. Anything. Everything. We will start over again in another country. Another world. A secret place without any of these monsters. We will live in a house where we can hide. They'll never find us. We will live on love and spend the rest of our lives in each other's arms. Tell me right now that you don't want this?'

He looks so sad, I don't know what to do. He has decided that he will send me away. I have no choice but to leave. He doesn't want me back. It is this wretched place where we began our love and this very same wretched place where we will end it.

The hangover from this sadness will never fade, I think. I am drunk, forever drunk, on all the things I never said to him.

'Pain can't tell the difference between good and bad. You can be the kindest soul and it'll still come after you like death.'

'Don't ask me to leave,' I moan. 'I can't do it.'

'Herga is not safe for you. As long as you stay here she will not spare you. And I am not powerful enough to stop her.'

'I love you!' I begin to cry. 'Doesn't that mean anything to you?'

There is a long pause. 'Everything. It means everything to me.'

I think the universe is terrified of us. Given a chance to redo something at all it will go back in time and change our paths so that we never meet. Or maybe I'm wrong. Maybe this is exactly what it wants. Maybe it's a sadistic universe. I don't know.

'The universe can't stop people from loving each other. But it can stop them from being together. And my my, how well, just how very well it does that,' he says.

I am so scared for us now.

'How can I just let you go like that?' I ask.

'Listen to me, Noor. There's no other alternative. You believe me, right?'

I nod. There's a long pause and he looks away.

'So this is it?'

'This is it.'

It's all happened too fast. I see him watching me from the window, and then, fighting those ghosts with his wolves. I see him standing in front of me now, his hands letting me go. A supercut. A library book. Another story that bites the dust.

I plead a while longer, but it's clear that he doesn't want me there. So I finally say in defeat, 'Will you keep in touch with me?'

He doesn't answer.

'So I leave with nothing?'

'Love. You leave with love.'

'And loss.'

He is quiet again.

'I'll never forget you,' I sniff, wiping my tears. I am trying to smile, trying to be brave, but I can't stop my heart from breaking. I am scared he might hear it. Look how things have turned out. We're crashing down. I think of how in an alternate reality, we'd be sitting in a cafe in London or New York or under warm bed sheets in Himachal or Ooty, and we'd have long conversations about Kierkegaard and Foucault and maybe share a cup of hot chocolate over musings about Salvador Dali and Monet. We'd watch snow from a cabin in the woods and make bonfires and marshmallows. We'd have picnics in gardens and read books to each other and make art, lots and lots of art. We wouldn't have to even dream of running away from evil forces and his fingers, by then, would have been washed off black magic from all the kisses I plant on them. We will camp under the stars and dance in the rain and watch the sunrise on the shore, his hand in my hand, his cheek against my cheek, sharing an earphone and listening to our favourite songs. No more ghosts to haunt us, Kalki, I think. No more fear. I don't ever want to look back. If only he'd come away with me and begin what should have started long ago in a new place. A place where we might be allowed a little joy, if we dared.

But happiness is a liar of a word. There isn't enough happiness in this world. That is what the real wars are for, the ones between countries, the ones between people. By the end of the day all of us want to be happy, even if it means putting someone else's happiness at stake. But life is such an unfair stretch of time. It tricks us, fools us, plays us. Because not all of us get to be happy. Not all of us know how to be.

He leans forward, acute. 'Let me tell you something, Noor. You're going to make it. I'm going to make it. We are all going to make it. It might be in pieces, but we will still make it. That's just how life is. You can live without me and I can live without you and I know it'll kill you for a long time before you can get up again and revive yourself. That's the beauty of the human soul. We trip and fall and sometimes we are caught by people and they make us fall again. One day you are going to realize that there won't be someone to catch you. And then, you will catch yourself. You will be the arms that hold yourself, the hands that pat your back, you will be the shoulder you cry on and the feet that carry you. You will keep going, Noor, because this is just one ending. It is not the end. In a parallel universe we are still always getting up. In all these parallel universes we fall and we get up in different ways. One moves to a different city, one stays up drinking the pain away every night, one paints, one cries to sleep, one remembers, one forgets, but one never dies. Noor, I have faith in you and I believe you can move on from all of this.'

'What if I don't? What if I'll never find someone like you?'

He smiles at me and tucks my hair behind my ear. 'I am already jealous, Noor, that you will get to spend the rest of your life with yourself. What I'd give to spend my life with you.'

My heart is mosaics on the interior now. Were we then part of a cruel dream? What of beautiful mistakes, are they life lessons that will scar us for evermore?

'Why are you doing this?' I ask once more.

'Because if I don't she'll kill you.'

I'm crying again. I am going to miss him. God, I am going to miss him.

'Let's talk about it,' I say. 'Can you walk with me outside and spend some more time with me? I need to clear my head. And yours.'

'Don't talk me out of it, Noor.'

'I won't.'

Something tells me he wishes I would. How did this happen, all of a sudden? Everything was fine, and now, now my life is at risk. I'm being hunted down and I can't stay in this place anymore.

'There should be some way out of this.'

'Is there?' he asks.

'Can't you come away with me?'

'The minute I leave she will come after me.'

'We can fight her.'

'She's still too powerful. She isn't going to spare

me. And if she sees you with me she isn't going to spare you either.'

'I don't know what to do.' I cover my face with my hands.

'Come. Let's go for a walk.'

The night is a rise of periwinkle and cadet.

Tornado shears into my palms. I want to place them on his cheek, slap him, fight him, tell him I hate him, love him. That I can't do this, that I need him. I am harvesting anguish on my chest, inhaling his love and exhaling heart break.

'What's this walk going to be about?' I ask.

'You know the answer.'

We aren't even in his room. I can't claw and break into him and into fits. I need to remain calm and composed. Strangers watch my parchment cheeks take in tears like accepting old wounds.

'Did you never see it coming?' he asks me. 'We were so happy, happier than anyone else in this world. Such happiness always has a price to pay.'

'I feel like someone has ripped a part of me. A half of me.'

His wolves are walking behind him like an army. One of them nudges me and whimpers. I bend down and pat his head. 'I'm leaving an entire family of the dearest hearts behind,' I say looking at them and remembering how they saved me. 'Thank you,' I whisper. 'For protecting me.'

'Come away with me,' I say one last time, but I know it's futile.

He puts his hand around me. 'If only it were that easy.'

The sky remains reserved and indifferent. A flavour of ice. A salvation from heat waves, a cool Neptune of cloud bursts. Denim and cornflower. The clear trail of regal blue tang. The stars, oh how they're laughing at us. You fools, they think. Nothing can stay happy for long under us. Every spotlight lasts but for mere seconds and we have had ours.

Now it is the time to grieve. To shed glow like snakeskin, to dim radiance until it becomes a dot, to lose our shine. And in that moment I realize, nothing can comfort my soul.

The pain of loss is crushing me. I've never known a hurt like this before. It sears into me and the moon can only watch and mourn for me. It can only put a blanket of night over us and ease us.

We wipe the prices of broken hearts from ourselves only to bleed right back into the same places.

Chapter Twenty

'I want you to love me again tonight,' I say. 'A little longer, a little harder. So that it feels closer to eternity. Even though I know it isn't. Please, just hold me.'

We are a macrocosm of tears, hiding from each other our heavy hearts, because we know it will hurt the other. I know he wouldn't want to see me sad so I keep throwing him smiles. But he knows me too well. Who am I trying to fool?

'Is there no other way?' I ask again.

His fingers are digging into my head, supporting me, breaking my fall. 'Who will catch me now?'

'You will have to,' he says.

Fever spreads rings around me. A kind of rocking ache harassing our already downtrodden hearts. It took poetry, coffee, midnight laughter and early morning conversations to get here. And it will take a whole brimstone of aeons to wash it all away.

'I love you so much, Kalki,' I say. 'You're going to rot in hell for loving me and leaving me like this.'

He breaks down all of a sudden and I jump. Holding him tight like a baby. I whisper to him, 'Please don't do this.' I kiss the top of his head. 'Don't cry, darling. We'll be okay.'

He's crying and I'm crying too. The flame lilies, they don't make a sound. There is only one tune left for them. One choir, one chord of finality.

And even they don't want to listen to sad songs. They turn their ears away and drown in their seas. Everything is drowning. Everything.

It is all over and we are washed upon the shore. There is nothing left except water in our lungs.

And still a little bit of love to spare.

Always a little bit of love to spare.

*

Tender morning oils over land. Sleep climbs onto eyelids like vines growing over trees and it pulls them down. But it is a new day and the farmers must go to work. The fields are calling.

Even when we stand no chance we fight for it. Are we being brave or are we being fools?

'Ah, but love makes fools out of all of us anyway,' he says. 'This world you have gifted me, Noor, is more magical than any magic I have known. And your love, it is more powerful than any magic in this world. You've bewitched me and there is nothing I can do but fall into your spell. And here I was thinking that I'm the magician.'

I smile. He has changed me. This beautiful, raw, shamelessly passionate man has changed me. There is no looking back now.

'I'm asking you one last time,' I say, 'if you say it, if you just say it, I am yours, Kalki. Please. I don't want to go back to Kashmir. Or to London. I want to spend the rest of my life with you.'

'You know why you can't, Noor.'

I begin to cry. He comes up to me and tries to hug me, but I push him away. 'I'll make sure she doesn't do that to me. Mind power helps, I swear! I can keep her out of my head. I promise you I'm not going near that well. Please, Kalki, please. *Please.*'

'Do you even know what I am?' He grabs me by the shoulders and shakes me hard. I've lifted my clenched fists from my eyes. 'You don't know! You don't know the half of it. What if all the spirits that are after me come after you too?' He turns around and curses loudly. 'You don't know how badly you're going to get hurt because of me. God, this should never have happened at all.'

'Don't say that, Kalki, please.' I run to him and hold him. My hands are all over him, but he doesn't respond. He just stands there. 'Don't leave me, please.'

'Please, Noor. Just go away.'

I take a step back but I don't stop crying. 'I'm never going to forget you.'

'May we meet again if there is another life,' he says. His eyes are dark clouds threatening to rain. But something tells me that this is how it's meant to be. We will never see each other again and we will burn in the hell of never seeing each other again. Sometimes this is how the universe wants it to be. It wants us to meet people who are special to us, but it also wants to teach us that nothing lasts forever.

'If we meet again I'll believe in magic,' he adds wistfully. 'The good kind.'

'Will you forget me?' I ask with a sad smile.

'I will try to forget you, Noor,' he says softly. His eyelids are umbrellas to his pouring eyes, but the rain never stops. 'But there will always be a part of me that's going to remember you when I see pretty smiles. When I smoke hookah or lie in my bed alone and empty. When I cross your Ajja's house. When I see old photos of you and Kirti. When I go to my underwater space. When I smell fresh daisies. When I see Kashmiri shawls. When I touch something, anything soft. Like your sunflower skin. When I see a painting. As beautiful as you. When I laugh, cry, blink, breathe. Yes. I am going to remember you for everything. Everywhere. Every time. Remembering you is like trying to remember how to breathe. I don't need to remember how to breathe. Remember is not an option, not a word. You will always be in me like pollens in flowers, only to be carried away to other flowers by the wind. When the wind comes you will be gone from my sight, but never from my heart. Never.'

I can't think anymore. I weep into his shirt and he lets me. I look up at him and say, 'I hate you.'

I kiss him one last time and it is over. As if it has always been.

And always will be.

And above us, the moon goddess wishes us luck. If it is our destiny, we will follow the stars back to each other. For as one, we're as stars, burning ourselves in the skies we're trapped in. We don't know any other way to be.

You will have to live without me, he says.

And you? What will you do?

Imagine a world without sun.

I'll never survive you.

Maybe. Maybe not.

*

In October I go back to London, after the house warming ceremony of our new house. It isn't as big as the old one, but we've adjusted with what we have. I convinced Baba to use the money he'd saved up for my marriage. I probably won't be getting married anyway. Or maybe I will, just to make Baba and Amma happy. But nothing is going to ever be the same. Nobody can replace him.

Daadi says, 'Noor *beta*, you've changed. Something about you is so different, I'm scared that place did something to you. I have never seen you this serious, this quiet, and you don't laugh at my jokes anymore. You're painting a lot, and you never paint at home. Are you missing London? I told you not to go to Herga. You never listen to me. You should listen to your elders.'

I want to tell her. Daadi, something happened. I saw ghosts and I stripped to my soul while astro projecting and I almost died inside a well. But that's not why I've changed. I fell in love and I'm not the same anymore. And I'm scared I'll never be the same. Ever again. I want to pour my heart out, but what do I say? Who will understand? Nobody will ever know what he was to me, and that secret will die with me.

After full day relaxations and shut downs, we have begun to see promise in Kashmir again. Perhaps it is just a pipe dream and the unrest will go on, but after all that's happened, I've learned that a little hope and belief gets us a long way.

But then, I remember him telling me that the saddest form of darkness is one that began in light. This is what hope can do to people. And I can't help but wish for things I'll never get.

In December, I write to Gopi and Arundhati, asking about him. They say that he's disappeared. Last I heard he's left the village and he's nowhere to be found.

They tell me he burned the house. And that he finally sealed the well. I wonder why. Why after all these years. I feel mad, betrayed for just a second. Why didn't he just get rid of the bracelet and fulfil his destiny? But a part of me knows. He probably did go insane with rage. I can't imagine anyone living in a place that's killed all the people they've ever loved. Or maybe losing *us* changed his mind about the village. When I left him he was a man with nothing left to lose, or so I'd believed. But now I don't know what this means. If he's shut down the well, does this mean the village is slowly going to rot?

The end is nearing, I can tell. A man has walked out of his hometown, leaving it in destruction. I don't know why, but my sense of betrayal settles into pride. I'm glad he's finally found the courage to set himself free. For himself if not for me.

Now he's at the mercy of Rakteswari. But I'd like to think he can hide himself well. And if I dare dream any further, I'd like to think he can fight back and perhaps even defeat her.

Nobody knows what has become of him. But they pray for him, just as I do. I hope wherever he is he's okay.

I've been reading a lot, my love, I imagine telling him. If I ever meet him again I want him to know how much I have learned from him.

If something is to stay in the memory it must be burned in: only that which never ceases to hurt stays in the memory. I love this. Nietzsche says it and Nietzsche is Kalki's favourite. If only I'd known how much this made sense back then. He is burned into my memory so badly. And the wound is still so raw.

I am the wound. And healing is unfathomable.

London too is not the same anymore. Wherever I go I dream of him. I paint him, on every piece of paper I get — the sun gleaming on his face as he makes circles in the water, the time we kissed in front of the tinkling temple bells, when we sat surrounded by our family of wolves, the night we made love under the streaming moonlight and when we came undone with the waves, the fireflies nestling in his god-like face and all the times when we bloomed like flame lilies.

I want him to see my world, of museums and towers and life outside the village. A life of exposure. It is painful to think of all the alternate realities that live. *If* is a rabid word.

I tell him about London life, the one we could have had, in my dreams. And I tell him in my lonely bed, longing for an impression on the pillow next to me, that we are happy here, in our little apartment and winter sun.

I think to him, wherever he is. *You're making breakfast in bed and the blender isn't working, so you say, baby, let's go out today, it's Paris and the air is so fine, je t'aime.*

I see your windblown hair undone from the hair band, loosening itself in the light cold and breathing its own beat. I want to hold you under Eiffel towers of stars and tell you I've found better skies down on earth. Your soul is exploding into mine like the fourth of July. But the thing about fireworks is that they're self-destructive. I am constantly losing myself in you and that will be the death of me.

But every time I wake up feeling like a late Sunday evening I can't help but remember our beautiful love affair stuck in the base of my throat like something I could neither swallow nor spit out. It was not a dainty summer thing. It was a stray hot air balloon floating out into space, a midnight in Venus, standing on top of London's Shard and late brunch in Nando's kind of insanity. It was your hand in mine, finger to finger, saying we could do this forever. Such lovable fools we were. We thought we could last. But we deserve to be remembered, my love. After all, we were a celebration. We were explosives. We were tragic. We knew nothing. We saw the best of times before it turned to ashes.

We were the brightest of fireworks. We shot straight up into the air like a summit, a crescendo, a grand finale before we burned to the ground.

Never again, my love.

It is the year of art exhibitions, a year that witnesses trees in full bloom. London, city of dreams, is most lively, and I have moved out of Maggie's place to my own in Piccadilly. This year I am hosting an art show with the income from selling my old art pieces. I have a few art collectors interested in my work. And a few connections and art dealers who sound promising.

Tonight, I am getting ready to light the beginning of an era of eerily haunting stories told by paints, flooding onto canvas the most silent of tales, the ones that are stepped on, marginalized and unrevealed. The histories that are never told. The romances that are never heard of. Today, as I wear my black lace dress and heels, I know I am awaited in a marvellous gallery that hosts my artwork, the ones that speak with thunder and fire bomb voices about a black magician who was a good man.

He still beats within me like a swan song, a tale past bed time, a recurring dream. A resonance of slow deaths.

It is so mesmerizing, isn't it? The concept of people as memories. The most breathtaking moments are people and moments are fleeting. If they are to be made eternal, we must let people go.

And that is what I have to do, let him *go*.

*

It has been months since the art show. There have been a few group exhibition offers and I am working on wall sized pastels. London has begun to feel like home again. I talk to my parents more often, they have all settled into the new house. I want to believe I too feel more settled. I have fewer dreams now. And I am back in the routine of my art class, blending in the browns.

'You must branch out, Noor,' I hear Chloe's voice drift over my bridged paper.

I gaze into my canvas, following the ebbing and flowing river of brown, dark curls against the sharp jawline. Fireflies. Wolves. A red *sari*. Flame lilies. A beautiful boy with kohl eyes.